I Pressed On

Atlantis Brown

I Pressed On Copyright © 2021 by Atlantis Brown.

All rights reserved. This book or any portion thereof may not be reproduced or used in any manner whatsoever without the express written permission of the publisher except for the use of brief quotations in a book review. Printed in the United States of America.

First Printing

ISBN# 978-1-943284-93-1 pbk

ISBN # 978-1-943284-94-8 ebk

A2ZBooks Publishing Lithonia, GA 30058 www.A2ZBooksPublishing.net. Manufactured in the United States of America A2Z Books Publishing has allowed this work to remain exactly as the author intended, verbatim.

*To my boys La'Daveon and David never doubt my love that
I have for you both. From the moment you were born you both
opened my heart and truly made me become a better woman.
I cannot promise to be here the rest of your lives but
I can promise to love you the rest of mine.*

Love always,

Mom

Table of Contents

Introduction vii

Chapter 1: Unreal Love 1

Chapter 2: Telling 13

Chapter 3: Unprotected 29

Chapter 4: Finding Me 35

Chapter 5: A Good Girl Gone Bad 45

Chapter 6: Earth Angel 59

Chapter 7: Turning Point/ Plot Twist 83

Chapter 8: Gracefully Broken 109

Chapter 9: Ready For Overflow 127

A Word to my sisters 135

About the Author: 137

Introduction

Depression will make you feel pain differently than other people. It is a serious mental illness that interfered with my life. On this day, I take in the memory of my past. I can vividly remember the thought that went through my head, "What are you doing girl? You have two boys; you are being a bit selfish. Just Let Go!"

I open my eyes and stared up at the ceiling. I swallowed, trying to push the nerves back down my throat. My eyes wet with tears; I began to unwrap the sheet from around my neck.

A great sob escaped me. I covered my face with shaking hands as the sound of wailing and suffering echoed throughout the hotel room. At that moment I sensed God's presence with me inside the hotel room. My body was filled with chills.

Although, He was not there physically; He was there spiritually. This is the day that God and His angels were in a spiritual battle over my life. At that point, I was exhausted. I had given up on life completely and was ready to throw it all away. I had been carrying this load of problems that were weighing heavily on my soul.

Most times, whenever I was upset, I often deal with my problems and keep them bottled up inside me. Can you identify with this? Who can you really talk to when you find yourself in this kind of situation?

You surely cannot talk to the person who made you feel that way. For me, I try to remain neutral. So, if anyone asks, I'll simply reply, "Oh I'm okay!" Putting on that fake smile, or I would also respond, "I'm well, how about you?"

Have you pretended to be happy so that no one knows the truth about how sad and depressed you really are? I did this all the time. Those that truly know me call me Laney and would say I am a great and fun person to be around.

I am always joking or making others laugh. I have always been a huge empath for others and would help fix their problems. I knew exactly what it felt like but I just could not deal with everything that I had going on in my life.

This was a way to keep myself going instead of thinking about my problems or having to deal with the issue at hand. I am what you call a super dedicated unpaid actress. Behind my smile, there was a breaking heart. Behind my laugh, I was truly falling apart.

Behind my eyes were tears at night. Behind my body is a soul trying to fight. I would pretend as if everything was great, but you can only pretend for so long. My body was weary, and I was very exhausted.

Things were driving me crazy and I was stressed out completely. I was battling depression and I did not even know it at the time. How did I get to this point you wonder? Well, let us go back to the early years of my childhood where I feel it all began.

Chapter 1
Unreal Love

Who knows what a good childhood really is? If you think for one second that having a good childhood simply means that you were given love and material things, you might be a little confused. I have criticisms for how I was raised, but I cannot deny that I was given things that most children did not have.

Early in my life like any other child, I was innocent. I was happy being around certain people. I was quiet, shy, and very curious but sneaky. My problem started with my mother. A daughter is supposed to be one of the most beautiful gifts this world must give.

A mother is supposed to provide protection, unconditional love, and emotional regulation for her children. However, I felt neither. Speaking from experience, an unhealthy mother-daughter relationship can lead to a poor relationship with oneself, low-self-esteem, and self-criticism.

In fact, enjoying a healthy mother-daughter relationship from my mom could have been the cure for some of my problems. It was like some sort of latent childhood. I had real unresolved issues. I grew up with all boys in a household of a single mother with no father in the home. I was the only girl and the baby.

I had an older sister but never met her because she died from Cyanotic Heart Defect before I was even conceived. While care and concern from both parents are important, my dad was MIA. Up until the age of seven, I thought that my two older brother's dad was my dad, but that is a story for another day.

As adults would say this day in time, "Out of sight, out of mind," meaning if a child does not see a person or thing for that period, then the child would not think about it or would soon forget about it until it is back in their presence.

However, when my truth unfolded to be a lie, my uncertainty generalized to the point where I trusted no one, not even the outside world. Everything was a lie until proven to be true. Despite what family members had to say about my mom when I was in their presence and all the things I faced as a child, I still loved her unconditionally.

You could not tell me anything about my mother. I do not know what my mother's real issues were growing up, but I knew for sure something was not right. My mom had a lot of male friends and different men would stay over from time to time. She would always drink, and I did not like how it made her act.

I could remember going to different relatives or her friend's home every weekend and being left alone sometimes with my brothers a night or two throughout the week. Sadness filled my body every time I would watch my mom prepare for the club or when I had to get dropped off to another person's home while she went out.

The nights my mom did stay home, I got the opportunity to sleep in the bed alongside her and that gave me a great sense of security and made me incredibly happy. The nights we were home, she took two blue pills every night before bed. I was uncertain why she took them every night but was determined to find out.

One Wednesday I was busy playing mommy to my dolls when my mom got a call from one of her friends that she went out with when attending Big Boys. Little did she know my mom was a couple of steps ahead of her because her outfit was laid out on the bed already. My face saddened when I heard her saying she was going but unfortunately this is something that I already knew.

I just wished I could have my mom all to myself. I stopped playing with my dolls and began to follow up behind her hoping she would stay but I knew that wasn't possible. I began to think, why does she have to always go out to the club? Why couldn't we just stay home on the weekends?

What was the difference between the nights in the week and the weekend? Why couldn't I wake up in my bed on a Saturday morning dumping out my bucket of toys at 6 am? Waking up to breakfast Saturday mornings. Instead, I had to be at someone else's home playing by their rules.

I know that one thing for certain; staying at my grandma's or uncle and aunts' home I was assured to have just that! I never said anything to my mom because as a child you did not have any wants. I watched as she ran herself an all hot bath. She turned on her stereo and listened to PPW on magic 97 while waiting for the water to cool down.

When she got into the tub, I hopped in right with her. While in the tub, she would always ask about my pocketbook. My pocketbook was another name she called my private part. She would point to what was really my vagina. She would say, "Don't let anyone mess with your pocketbook; nobody is supposed to be messing with your pocketbook. You tell me, Okay!"

Because I was the timid type of girl, I would laugh and say, "Okay." But I really felt uncomfortable by her looking and pointing to it. I had no understanding as to why they were not supposed to be messing with my pocketbook. I would watch my mom take her bath and as soon as she got out of the tub, I would sit in her spot and bath my body the exact way she did.

While I bathed, I watched my mom dry herself off and put on her panties and bra. I watched her pull open the secret mirror to get her curlers out to plug up. I instantly thought about the blue pills. I pulled the stopper out of the tub and got out to dry my body off. I put on my clothes and went into the kitchen to get a cup from the drying rack next to the sink.

I walked back to my mom's room with the cup and stuck only my head in to see where she was. I did not see her in the room, so I knew she had made her way back to the bathroom to curl her hair. I hurried and placed the cup under her bed where it was not visible. My heart beating rapidly, I went into the bathroom and pulled down the toilet seat.

I took a seat and watched my mom curl her hair with the hot curling iron. After curling her hair, she made me get in my bed. She got dressed for the club and put on her red lipstick to match and left quicker than she could pop her lips. I shared a room with my older baby brother, and it took him no time to fall asleep.

When he started snoring, that was my cue. I got up and went into my mom's room, bent down and looked under the bed for the cup. I grabbed the cup from under her bed and ran into her bathroom closing the door. I filled my cup with water and placed it on the toilet seat. I stood up on the toilet making my way on top of the sink. I opened the mirror and found the pill bottle.

I tried twisting the top several times, but it did not open. I started to get frustrated a bit. Hmm. Why was it not opening for me? I grunted angrily and pushed down hard on the top and twisted like I watch my mom do and it finally opened. I sighed with relief. I took two of the pills out and placed them on the sink along with the open pill bottle.

I jumped down from the sink putting the two pills in my mouth. I swallowed them and took a sip of the water. Shortly after taking the pills, I began to feel a dull, aching pain in my chest. I got scared because I knew something was not right, so I drunk the remaining water that was left in the cup and that made me feel a little better, so I thought.

I went got in my bed and before I could even pull the cover back, I was off to sleep. The next morning my mom came to wake my brother and I up, but it was so hard for me to get up. I felt like I was hit by a hurricane; I felt dizzy, my head was hurting, and my vision was blurred. I had a hard time getting ready that morning.

I felt sluggish and everything was going in slow motion, including myself. The bus horn blew, and it was time for me to go. Lucky thing I was in Head Start. My teacher thought that I went to bed late and brought out a cot for me to lay on. I slept the majority of that whole day. They tried waking me up for lunch, but I still was restless.

I took one bite of my food and threw up. Talking about feeling bad, I felt horrible. I knew one thing for sure the blue pills were not for kids like me and I would never want to take a pill again in my life. It made me very sleepy and I did not like how it made me feel. My teachers called my mom and told her about me not feeling well. She cleaned me up and put me back on to my cot for the rest of the day.

It is true enough that all daughters of unloving and attuned mothers have common experiences. The lack of that motherly warmth and the wanting of validation warps their sense of self. How come I was not enough for her? Did I do something wrong? All I wanted was approval and love from my mom, but my mom was seeking approval and love from someone else.

One day my uncle introduced her to one of his cousins. They must have hit it off good because it was not long before he had begun to stay the night a lot. I did not like it one bit and there was something about him that I did not like. Maybe it was the fact that he would be taking up the time that I barely did get with my mom and I was jealous. Or maybe it has something to do with me seeing him for the no-good nigga he truly was.

As a kid, I observed everything closely. I paid attention to how he would always have to get up and smoke a cigarette all the time. He would sweat and it was not even hot in the house. The man would not sit still for one minute and as a kid, it was making me nervous.

Why wasn't my mom telling him to sit his ass down like she would do to me? It was like he was hiding something but hey I was only a kid. I was one to never speak my mind, but my thoughts would be saying a hell of a lot.

The fact that I already did not get the time like I wanted with my mom was majority of the issue. I never got a good feeling with him being around. However, her having a boyfriend slowed her down because she did not go out as much, which was how I liked it. Her focus was more on him though.

We would visit her friends more often and she slowed down on going to the club which was also okay with me because I got the chance to be around more instead of always being dropped off. I think part of the reason why we visited her friends more was to show off her new man. One day my mom went over to one of her friends' home.

Before we exited the car, she was talking to her boyfriend. He had her blushing and laughing. I rolled my eyes and I opened the car door to get out, it made me sick to my stomach. I looked around and saw a lady with golds in her mouth smiling and walking from under the carport.

I looked around and saw there were a bunch of men standing around this Cadillac in the front yard laughing and talking loudly. One man with a jerry curl was staring at me oddly. I looked back at him because I was wondering why his head looked like a bunch of wet shiny black ramen noodles. I felt my stomach churning and begin to knot. I did not think much of it though.

The lady began to walk towards me and she signaled for my mom to get out of the car. My mom and her man exited the car and began to walk over to the crowd of men. My mom spoke to everyone along with her boyfriend and introduced him to everyone. The lady said, "Come on Lania, let me take you to meet my granddaughters!"

She grabbed me by the hand and led me to the car porch where her granddaughters and a couple more children were. I stood there quietly looking at the kids. The girls began talking to me and I would only answer if they asked a question. They all began putting their foot in a circle.

One girl said, "Put your foot in and you can hide with me." I walked over and put my foot in the circle. They picked the tree as the base and explained the rules to me because this was all new to me. I began to feel comfortable and the knots in my stomach began to ease up.

This was out of my norm because I usually would be up under my mom all the time when I explore a new place. Running around so much made us thirsty. The girls went in to get them a juice and I followed behind to get one for myself also. I asked the girl to use the bathroom. She told me to follow her and led me to the back down a hall where the bathroom was.

I went inside to pee. When I was done, I wiped myself and flushed the toilet. I walked to the sink, turned on the water and washed my hands. That feeling in my stomach had begun to come back. It felt like I almost had to do number two. I turned off the water and walked towards the door.

I opened it and the man with the jerry curls was standing at the door. I was scared out of my mind like I had seen the devil himself standing right before me. I tried to hurry past him and he picked me up and placed his hand over my mouth. I began kicking and screaming.

He laid me on the bathroom floor and took a knife out of his right pocket. He opened it and place it on my neck. He said, "I will put this knife right through your neck and watch you bleed to death if you say one word." My eyes widened and I was thinking where the others were. Please do not hurt me.

He removed his hand and I shouted, "Help!" He poked the knife hard up against my neck. I told him I want my momma please; he placed his finger over his lip. Tears began to stream along my face. He turned on the water and began letting it run. He slapped me and told me to hush angrily. His eyes were red and big.

He began unbuckling his silver plate on his belt, unzipping his pants removing his penis. He removed the knife from my neck placing one hand there while touching my pocketbook. He inserted one finger into my pocketbook. Tears began streaming down my face. His nail was scratching me.

The words of my mother began to play over in my head. "Don't let nobody mess with your pocketbook; nobody is supposed to be messing with your pocketbook. You tell me, Okay!" He began putting two fingers into my pocketbook. Inserting them inside and out. The pain I felt was excruciating.

He laid on top of me trying to put the tip of his overly large penis into my baby vagina. I got nauseous and overheated. A lady said, "Is there someone in there I got to pee. His hands covered my mouth quickly. Footsteps began walking down the hall a bit further. He pressed his hands up against my mouth and put the knife back to my neck.

He was nearly smothering me laying on top of me. I felt like I was going to suffocate. He told the lady, "I needed more tissue." He said, "I'm coming for you in your dreams you better not say one word." I got up and ran out of the bathroom towards the outside door. I was trying to gasp for air. I wanted my momma.

I ran out the door outside to my momma. I was scared out of my mind. When I made it outside, I ran to the end of the car porch. There was a group of adults outside around her and I needed to get her alone. I was high yellow and by the look on my face, you could tell I had been crying. She said, "What's wrong with you?"

Everyone looked at me and it made me feel uncomfortable. I was embarrassed and scared. I replied, "I got to pee!" Well go pee, don't come being up under me," she replied. I felt rejected and did not know what to do. "Come on baby, I'll take you!" I looked up to see the evil man smiling. Holding that same knife, he had up to my neck.

I took off running to our white topaz, opened the door and got in the car. I locked all the doors. I laid down on the red/burgundy looking seats. I was so scared and filled with so many emotions and I did not know what to do. I began crying and balled up tightly like a butterfly stuck in its cocoon.

I was quiet the rest of the car ride home. When we made it home it was bedtime. I waited for my mom to take her a bath. She ran her water all hot like always. I gathered my clothes from out my drawer and walked into her room to take them to her bathroom. She said, "You are getting too big to be bathing with me go to the other bathroom and take you a bath."

I felt embarrassed because she said this in front of her boyfriend. I turned around and went to the other bathroom to run some bathwater for myself. I took off my clothes, I looked down at my underwear to see brown stains on them from dried up blood. I got into the water and sat down in the water and my pocketbook began to burn.

I'm talking about the Alicia keys song, "This girl is on fire!!" But seriously, this pocketbook was burning. I screamed. It hurt so badly and I could not sit in the water. I began to cry, and I screamed, "Momma!" I called out her name until she came. It brought tears to my eyes and made my nose run; it hurt so badly. When she came into the bathroom I was still crying and hollering.

She said, "Is the water too hot?" I said my pocketbook; it burns and hurts. "She hollered, "Get out of the damn tub, I told you not to be putting soap in your pocketbook. It doesn't go down there." While snatching me out of the water. I said, "I didn't put it in my pocketbook. It was the evil man!" She grabbed a towel and said, "Dry yourself off and get in the bed."

I looked at her as she walked away and out the door. I saw my brother looking to see what was going on. I was completely embarrassed and hurried and shut the door. I dried off and put on my clothes then went to bed. I thought now what is the point in letting her know about someone messing with my pocketbook if she was going to ignore me and not do anything?

My brother Brandon was so annoying, he was laughing and making fun of me. Repeatedly saying "You a cry baby!" I got heated and angry. He kept pushing my buttons, so I got up from the bed and was ready to fight. I pushed him and he got his pillow and started hitting me with it.

My mom came out from her room and with a belt. She was cursing and hollering.

She gave me two licks and I fell to the ground kicking and screaming. She hit me a couple more times again and said, "Cut all that out!" I screamed at her and said, "I want my granny!"

I felt alone and hurt. That day really shook me up and I did not know what I could do. I just needed to rest but my nights became restless and I did not get any good rest for a while. In fact, I even began to have nightmares. All I could think about was the evil man coming to get me in my sleep so I would try to stay up majority of the nights.

I was thinking about the two blue pills to help make me rest, but I did not want to deal with the effects of the medicine after waking up. I was yearning for that maternal warmth, love, and protection. Yet, despite this painful experience, it was the first of many. My mother had ignored a lot and she was always unavailable.

This left me feeling abandoned and with special scars of their own. All my mother's behavior did was leave me emotionally hungry and sometimes desperately needy. I began to accept the fact that my mom was unavailable and began to turn to my older brothers which helped but it did not really heal the scar that my mom left.

Atlantis's Advice:

If you are ever in a situation and you are uncertain, always go with your gut feeling. This is one tangible and hard feeling to describe, but it is often held to be true. I always got this feeling as a kid, even now when something was not right. I would always get knots in my stomach that were painful. Somewhere deep down inside there would always be this feeling of hesitancy or uncertainty.

If I failed to detect a problem or articulate the wrongfulness I would always feel, I often went ahead with my actions because sometimes I just think it's me being fearful. Intuition allows you to get the first warning when something is off. If you ever have a gut feeling that something is not right, listen to it. A lot of times we do not trust people and some things may be inaccurate, but this is something you need to pay attention to and not ignore.

To the parents:

You have nothing in this world more precious than your children. No matter what you may be going through, you can always find love in your children. Do not trade your motherhood for some bauble of passing value because your children did not ask to be here. From the time your child is birthed into this world, they will grow quickly and you may never get back the time you miss out with them.

Your children did not ask to be here, so do not put your problems or the wrongful choices you made on their shoulders expecting them to carry the load. Children look up to their parents, so model the person you would like them to become because they look up to you.

Chapter 2
Telling

My mother had changed a lot since she got her new boyfriend. Most of the changes were good I would say, but then when things would be sour with him, she was back to her old ways. She was somewhat paying attention to her children, but majority of her focus was on him. Children indeed know the energy of other people and they know when a person is not right.

I did not like him; in fact, I had hatred for him. When he would be around, I would get that feeling in my stomach. I wondered if he would try to hurt me like the evil man. I did not know what to think and I was desperate to leave and go to my aunts and uncles every weekend. I wanted to tell them because even at a young age, it was weighing heavy on my mind.

I was really scared because if my mom ignored me then why would anyone else believe me. I was only a kid and there was nothing I could do, so I just let it be, but that did not stop it from bothering me. The only place I felt safe was at home in my room playing with my dolls and annoying brother or my aunt and uncles.

It was not long before my mom announced that we would be moving. We were in search of a new house and was going to leave 1605 behind. I was hurt at the fact that we were leaving because our neighbors were like family. How could we leave our family behind? All my mom had to say was, "I'm getting tired of living in a rat-infested house."

Moving day had come sooner than I expected. I went to stay over at my aunt's place for the weekend. When most of the furniture had been moved to our new four-bedroom house, I came back home. My two older brothers had their room and I was stuck in the room with the most annoying sibling of them all. I made the most of it because he was nice to me sometimes.

I walked around the house and saw that boxes and things were still everywhere. My mom said to me, "I don't need you in the way, I'm trying to get everything arranged properly so stay out of my way." The way she would come off so harsh really hurt my feelings. I was extremely sensitive, and it did not take much to hurt my feelings, but I played tough. I did not say a word and just walked out the front door. My mom made me feel like I was a bother to her, and it made me feel like I was nothing, nor did I mean anything to her. I walked up from under the car porch down the driveway and stood midway. I looked around at my new neighborhood. I looked over to my right and saw a girl eating Cheetos. I instantly got hungry. I thought to myself man I want some of those Cheetos.

It took me some time but eventually, I walked over to the girl and stood by her while she was eating the Cheetos. I introduced myself and she asked me if I wanted some and we stood by the trunk of the car in her yard eating Cheetos. I had made a friend and it all started with the Cheetos. Every day I would go outside to play with my new friend.

I even began going to the same school as she and her siblings. I was hoping she and I would be in the same class, but she was way older than me. I was just beginning first grade and she was going to the fourth grade. My emotional hunger and need shifted from my brothers and moved over to her and her mom. I was trying to get over what that evil man had done to me and enjoy the motherly warmth I got from being around my friend and her mom.

I soon stopped wanting to visit my aunts and uncle because I had exactly what I needed close to home. I was starting to be my happy self again. I was even okay with the fact that my mom had a boyfriend. I mean he did stick around longer than others. He even got a job in the cafeteria at my school. I thought it was embarrassing but I liked the idea of having a father figure in my life.

He never tried anything like the evil man, so guess he was okay. I think he was beginning to become comfortable with me also and started calling me, "Mrs. Buttercup." I did not like it because it made me think that he was only being nice for something, and I was not used to people being nice. I think he paid attention to the fact that I watched a lot of power puff girls.

One day I asked him, "Why do you call me Mrs. Buttercup?" He said, "Both of you have the same personality." I asked, "How?" He replied, "You're a straight-up tomboy and ain't nothing girly about you. You go toe to toe, and you got heart and ain't scared of nothing." I did not know what to say. Little did he know that I was terrified of everything, but I had to be tough or get run over.

He reached out his fist to give me some dap. I smiled and dapped him up. I was beginning to think that the dude was okay after all. I felt a bit uncomfortable, but this was all because I had low self-esteem. I was used to my brothers calling me ugly or telling me stories about how

I was adopted because I was brighter than them. They would tell me horrible stories.

I felt negative about myself at such a young age. I would get compliments from my uncle, grandma, or mostly strangers. I did not believe them though because I was always torn down by my brothers and I never heard words like "you're beautiful or I love you from my mom, ever! I felt a little more confident by hearing him speak positively about me.

I started to feel calm and content with everyone and everything in my life. We would have family gatherings at our house from time to time. I enjoyed having everyone over, playing with my cousins and my new extended family. One gathering we had I remember my mom and her boyfriend got into an argument after everyone left.

Their tones were not at a respectful level as they were hollering at the top of their lungs. They were all over the house with it and even outside. This was just embarrassing because we were new in the neighborhood. I went into the room I shared with my brother and shut the door. I sat on the floor in front of my twin bed.

This was not their first time arguing but being in a new house, I wonder where he would go because he gave up his apartment when we moved into this house. I was beginning to get worried and who was I going to turn to for comfort? My favorite brother (the second to the oldest was gone) and I despised my brother Brandon. He picked on me so much that I hated him.

I could not go over to my neighbor's house because I had never stayed the night. Eventually, it died down and he left. I was able to get myself relaxed and I got into my bed. We had a long day playing so I was very tired. Before long, I was sound asleep in my bed. I was woken up out of my sleep by the sound of shattered glass.

Sometimes the worst thing about feeling afraid is that you do not know what to do. I jumped up and went to my moms' room. I was thinking about the evil man. He had finally come to get me. I began to cry because I said I should've never gone to sleep. My mom was on the phone with the police. I began to get worried because I did not want anything to happen to my mom.

Would the evil man try to hurt her? After getting off the phone with the police, my mom called my aunt to come and pick us up. I was confused; I did not want to leave my mom and was worried out of my mind. The ambulance and the fire truck arrived first. My mom was upset and she kept saying, "This dude broke my windows."

There were so many emotions running through my body, and I did not understand why? On the other hand, I was a bit relieved that it was her boyfriend and not the evil man. Shortly, my uncle arrived but I did not want to leave my mom alone. I loved my mom with everything in me even though she was emotionally unavailable.

This was not fair and it made me wonder if I can ever enjoy my bed. I am always having to go here and there and I was so sick of it. I hopped in the truck and we drove back to their house. When we got inside the house, I went to my cousins' room and got in the bed. I could not sleep because I was too worried about my mom.

I could not wait to go back home and at least sleep in the bed with my mom again. Worry becomes a problem when it causes a problem. All I wanted to do was get back to my mom's. This stay at my aunts' home seemed the longest. My mom had to get the windows replaced. My cousins were starting to agitate me, but I had to remember that this was their home and not mine. I could not just do what I wanted to do.

Honestly, I just did not want to be bothered. I was profoundly grateful for my uncle and aunt because I was treated like one of their kids – without favoritism or difference. I was just fed up with not being able to stay at my home. I did not go home until after the windows were fixed and lasted for almost a week. The weekend came and I was so glad because I had one hell of a week.

On Friday, I played with my friend next door until late in the evening. We were truly getting close. I thought more of her as a sister and not my friend. I followed her all over the neighborhood. Whenever I was around her, it's always an opportunity for me to relax and not worry much. It was not long before her mom hollered out for her to get her butt in the house.

After she went in, I had no choice but to go back to my house. I bathed and went straight to bed. My mom still was not home, so I figured she went out. I woke up the next morning and decided to watch the television in the living room. My oldest brother came in and sat in there with me. He began to tickle and play with me and it made me feel a lot better because I was completely stressed out.

Both of us were not as close as my other brothers but that was because he was practically grown. He went from tickling me to putting me in his lap. I started to get a feeling of uncertainty, but he was still trying to tickle me, so I just thought he was playing. My mom would always say you do not sit in a man's lap. She never had to worry about me sitting in a man's lap because I now understood what she meant by nobody is supposed to mess with your pocketbook after what happened with the evil man.

When it came to my mom talking to me about certain things, she never did. A lot of the things that I knew were either the things I learned while watching TV, from experience, or heard from someone else. My brother started to play with me more often, but the more he would play with me the more uncomfortable I got.

He would sometimes try to pick me up and would rub me against his groin and it would be on hard. I began to tell him to stop, I do not like that, but it was like one word in one ear and out the other. I started to avoid him and also avoid wanting to go home. I also started having nightmares about the evil man and gradually became defiant with my teacher.

On weekends I would be ready to go over to my grandmother's house or my aunt's house. I was becoming really filled with anxiety and paranoid. I did not want him hurting my pocketbook just as the evil man did. He only did this when my mother was gone and I had nowhere to turn to. I would try to be up under my second to the oldest brother and he became my main protector.

He did not play about me at all, the only thing was he always running the streets or spending the night over his friend's house. Either way that still did not stop my oldest brother from trying to take advantage. One day I was lying down with the cover pulled up to my head while watching TV in my room.

My bedroom door creaked open and he came in and pulled his penis out of his pants and began to shake it. My heart sank and I just closed my eyes. I did not understand what was going on. "Put that thing away!" I shouted. Why is he doing this, I was his little sister? I was lying there silently scared out of my mind. I did not move a muscle and my heart began to race.

He sat down on the bed beside me and began to play with himself. I was completely disgusted by him. He pulled the cover back and I turned my head. He said, "Is it big?" I begin to silently scream. I was only seven years old. It was all becoming too much for me to handle. I did not fully understand as a child what an adult could want with a child.

After he ejaculated, he quickly placed his penis inside his pants and got up walking out of my bedroom door like nothing ever happened. I waited to get up because I was truly scared out of my mind. I heard the bathroom door close and I got up quicker than a bunny jackrabbit. I went to my moms' room and she was neither there nor in her bathroom.

I hurried and ran past the bathroom door where he was and looked in the living room and kitchen and she was not in there either. I did not even stop to put on a pair of shoes, I didn't care. I got up out of that house quickly. When I opened the door, my mom's car was outside, so I knew she had to be there. I checked the washroom outside, but she was not there.

I started walking to my neighbor's house. I saw my third oldest brother playing with my friends' brother. I asked him about momma and he told me she was across the street over our cousin's house. I walked over to our cousin's house to see my mom and our cousin drinking beer talking, having a good time.

I had to build up the courage while walking over there. I was scared, trembling, and my heart was pounding. I called her name, "Mama!" My mom dismissed me so quickly that if it were groundhog trying to turn around, it would not have seen its shadow. She said, "Leave me alone! Do not come over here bothering me."

My cousin said, "These grown folks talking, go and play with the kids." I was completely embarrassed and hurt. I replied, "I need to talk to my momma." "Whatever it is it can wait till I come home!" replied my mom. I felt rejected and let down for the second time. She did not even allow me to say anything.

I walked back across the street upset. I went and told my brother Brandon she was over there smoking a cigarette. My brothers were like the men of the house and she would always listen to them, so I knew she was in trouble. It made me feel a little better hearing him fuss at her since she had not listened to me. At this point, I began building up some resentment towards my mom.

I was her only surviving daughter. God took away my sister and here I was a second blessing and look at how I was being treated. I felt if this is how you treat your kids, then she should have not had any. I felt like I was better off somewhere else. I always saw how my friend's mom treated her and how my aunt and uncle treated my cousins and I wanted that type of treatment from her, but this lady was cruel to me at times.

The times I needed her the most. My mom would be nice around certain people. She would often talk about my sister but look at how she was acting with the one God gave her a second chance with. My mom did not tell me she loved me, I did not get hugs or anything. I was deprived of having a secure attachment. I always long for her attention but was completely ignored all the time.

I was scared and did not know what to do. I did not trust anyone all that much and I felt hopeless. I know my mom had love for me, but she did not know how to say or show it. No matter how many times you show or tell a person something, if she does not believe in herself then she will not believe you.

Somewhere along the way, my mom was lost and the problems of her past were becoming my reality. I began to feel like maybe I would be better off with my sister. I had to tell somebody because I just could not take again what happened to me with the evil man. My pocketbook was sore for days. Instead of bathing I took wash offs in the sink. Just the thought of the whole situation, I had to tell someone, and I had to do it quickly.

My brother would soon be graduating high school and would be off to college, so my plan was always to avoid him as much as I could.

It seems that my brother noticed that I was avoiding him. He got bold enough to come into the room while my mom would be in her room sometimes at night. It was like he did not care. I could not hide from him. I began to have murderous thoughts. I began to plan how I was going to murder him. This was beginning to be all too much for me, I am only a kid.

I felt like I could trust my friend a little. I decided I would tell her because I was tired and could not go on living like that. This was so hard for me to do. I feared the outcome. If he found out I told, what if he did something to me? I would often think about the evil man.

I said I would never take a pill again but eventually; I began taking those blue pills more because one day I would hope that I did not wake up. I was too young to be having these types of problems. What else could I do? I remember going to school one day and we had an officer come and talk to us about safety.

I felt like that was God speaking through the officer because he was saying if you were ever in trouble to reach out to him. I thought long and hard about raising my hand. I was too scared and embarrassed. I did not want the other kids to think that I was a snitch or even make fun of me. The fact that I did not know what the outcome would be scared me out of my mind. I knew that I had to do something because I could not endure how this was making me feel.

The only thing that had been on my mind that whole week was you must tell. So, the weekend was approaching, and I was tired. I was tired of running from the problem. When Friday came after school, I decided that I would tell my friend, but how was my main problem. That evening I was ready to go outside and be with my friend.

I was changing out of my jeans and spirit shirt. I heard somebody coming so I hurried and got under my bed. It was him. I was thinking.

I am so sick of this boy. I waited for a while under my bed. For a short time, I did not hear anything, so I got from under my bed. I put on my shorts; I peeked my head out my room door.

The coast was clear, and I made a run for it. I walked swiftly down the long hallway that seemed to never end. Before I could make it to the end, he was right there in front of me. He began asking me was it big and to touch it. I said, "I'm gone tell momma on you!" He grabbed my hand trying to make me touch him but I jerked away and ran towards the door.

He came behind me, but I was too quick for him. I had enough of him. How could you sexually abuse your little sister? He was a creep and I hated him. All I could think about was that he was supposed to be my protector. I hurried up and slammed the door running on the side of the house to the back yard. I did not stop until I made it to the canal ditch behind the house.

I let out a scream. I looked at the water in the canal ditch. I did not understand; why? Why me? Tears began to run down my cheeks. I thought of jumping into the canal but I didn't have the courage to jump. I looked back and I saw my friend playing in her front yard. I wiped my tears using my shirt.

I turned around and walked down the hill of the canal ditch and over into her yard. We began walking in the neighborhood. I did not talk much like I normally would because I was just thinking of how I was going to tell her. It was getting close to dark and I knew I did not have much time. I went back and forth with myself, but I was scared to tell her.

What if she did the same as my mom and ignore me, but she was my only hope. I began asking her questions about the situation and what she would do. Before I knew it, I had told her everything that was going on. She asked me why I did not tell my mom and I told her about me being too scared and how I was rejected.

She said, "Well I'm going to tell my mom." I said, "No!" I really wanted her to go and tell my mom for me because I did not have the courage to tell her and how she always would dismiss me. She assured me that everything would be okay. She came up with the idea of telling her mom and have her mom to tell my mom. I was okay with that.

I felt like a big weight had been uplifted off my shoulders. It was time for her to go inside and I asked her if I could stay the night. She asked her mom if I could but she said, "No because we lived right next door to one another and would see each other the next day!" Which was correct because I would come over almost every day.

My friend had informed me that she told her mom. I am not sure when my godmother had told my mom, but I remember sitting in Mrs. Olivia's 2nd-grade class doing the work that she had assigned. Mrs. Olivia had walked over to the door and called my name for me to step outside. She was our new teacher and I had not given her any problems that I knew of.

My heart began to beat rapidly. I did not want a paddling by Mr. Hill the school principal. I got up out of my desk and began walking towards the door where Mrs. Olivia was standing. She opened the door and motioned her hand telling me to go out. I walked out and she followed behind me. "I don't want to hear one word while I'm outside," said Ms. Olivia.

She closed the door and kneeled in front of me grabbing both my hands. I had the face of a sad puppy; I did not know what she was going to say to me. "Is someone bothering you?" she asked. "No," I replied. I thought about the situation with my brother, but I knew she was not talking about that because only God, my friend, her mom, and of course the perpetrator knew.

"Has anyone been bothering you at home?" I paused. Wait, why is she asking me this? How did she suspect this? "It's okay, Atlantis! I am here to help you. You can tell me. I promise to keep this between the two of us," said Mrs. Olivia. So many thoughts ran through my head, I was afraid that my brother would come for me; or try to harm my mom, brothers, or even me. I feared everything.

I looked into her eyes and they spoke to me at that moment. I knew that she was being honest with me just by looking into her eyes. "My brother!" I replied. She asked, "How long has he been sexually abusing me?" I told her he has been doing it for some time. I was scared to tell. I started to cry. All my emotions had come out at that very point.

She said, "Stay right here!" She went back into the classroom and came back with a box of tissue. Mrs. Olivia assured me that everything would be okay and did not have to worry about it happening anymore. She wiped my face with the Kleenex and wrapped her arms around me tightly. For the first time, I felt protected and safe right there in Mrs. Olivia's arms and I did not want her to let go of me because I was not sure what was next to come.

I did not return to the classroom. Mrs. Olivia held my hand and walked me to the office. I was greeted by Ms. Hamilton sitting at her desk. She was always nice and made you feel welcomed. Ms. Hamilton walked me into the office where the principal and a police officer was sitting. I began to feel many emotions that day. I was so scared.

After school that day we were all in the car except my second to the oldest brother because he was always with his friends. We made a quick stop at the WGG to get some gas. My mom gave my oldest brother the money to go pay for the gas. She got out of the car to pump the gas.

While standing at the pump she knocked on the window and told me to get out.

I was not sure why she wanted me to get out, so I did? When my oldest brother came out of the store, she asked me, "Has he been messing with you? I said, "Yes!" He was walking up behind my mother and told her, "I got it mom!" "Have you been messing with Laney?" My mom asked him. He replied, "No!" "Yes, he is!" My brother got very angry and said, "I will beat your ass. Don't you ever stand up there and lie on me. I don't do no shit like that."

I have never seen him get so upset like the way he got, but he was looking my mom dead in the face lying. I thought he was going to hurt me trying to jump over the pump cord. I did not understand, I was thinking so you are not the brother that comes into my room trying to make me watch you, touch you, ask me to do this and that? I was baffled.

"My mom said, "Calm down! I never said you did; I just asked a question." I could not believe that she was calming him down. All I remember thinking was why would you even ask me this in front of him. "Hold up! He is lying." This made him extremely angry. He got to cursing and making a big scene. My mom was being sensitive to his needs.

Not once did she say it was going to be okay Laney or I believe you! I am going to make sure this does not happen ever again. I was a kid and yes, I did some sneaky things but I'm not one to just lie. At that very moment, I knew I could not trust anyone. How could you stand up there and say you had not done anything with a completely straight face? I did not have my mother's protection, yet again.

I knew that I could not turn to her for anything. Little by little my soul had caught on fire. I realized at this moment I would have to face everything in this world alone. As a kid, I put up with everything my mom did. I forgave her with the blink of an eye for every time she would criticize me, talk harshly to me, or for all the times she neglected me when I needed her the most.

Although I often tried not to question the things she had done. I would always blame myself for everything, deep down knowing I did nothing wrong but that was my way of making the situation better. The one thing I feared the most was my mother abandoning me for good, but I learned to deal with those short absences, even though it was scary to me.

She was there physically part-time but emotionally, she was gone. At that very moment, the feelings that I had for my mother I felt as though they were gone. My mother was in complete denial. That was my brother I was talking about, her oldest and first-born child, to her he was the perfect son. He did well in school and was always so polite at home and to others.

He made her look like the perfect mother. He attended church and knew the bible front to back, but even demons pretend to be angels. I hated him with a passion. I thought brothers were supposed to be a sister's protector, at least that is what I was hoping for. I did not fully understand as a child what he was doing.

He started with something so simple as tickling me. Each time it would always be different and the more he would act as if he was playing with me, the more he was indirectly taking advantage of me. God blessed me with the spirit of discernment at an early age and I always knew when something was not right. My stomach got butterflies, my heart would always race, and my whole body would just feel uncomfortable.

My mom being unavailable all the time only made me more frantic. I believe that many people feel that girls and their emotions are like a natural pairing, but it is honestly not. Picture any kid being overcome with so many emotions and not even knowing how to deal with them; that makes you incapable. I never expressed any of my authentic emotions because my mom did not take me seriously. Crying to her was like a sign of weakness. It may sound weird, but I temporarily became a troublemaker. Since I could not get her love I settle for her anger.

Atlantis's Advice:

If you are ever in a situation like the one I was in, stop being afraid of what could go wrong. Do not let your fear make you become paralyzed. The reality of my fear was that I was not scared of my brother; I feared him trying to hurt me.

Parents: Good communication is important to any relationship. You should look at your child and smile at them. Show interest in what your child is doing. Pay attention and listen closely when your child talks to you. It is especially important that you show your children attention, no matter what age. The small things matter.

Emotional and social health is important to children because it helps them feel good about themselves, so when your child shows signs and may be acting differently, you will know that something is not right. I began to build up so much anger, I would hardly talk to anyone.

I had low self-esteem, and it was difficult for me to go to sleep at night, so I self-medicated myself with those blue pills. All the signs were there but because of other things going on with my mom she did not care to even notice. You should never leave your daughter around any man or boy because you just do not know people like you think you know them. The big problem was, Oh! They're not like that or they would never do this to my baby. Expect the unexpected always.

Chapter 3
Unprotected

I was glad that the burden of secrecy had been lifted but what do I do now? When sexual abuse takes place within families, the pain we experience can include conflicting and confusing emotions. We may feel extreme anguish over what has taken place to the child, while still feeling love and concern for the family member who also committed the abuse.

However, in my situation, after everything that happened initially with my oldest brother, nothing was solved. My mom continued like nothing ever happened. The sexual abuse stopped for a short time, but I was traumatized. I began to believe that it was my fault in a way. I felt ashamed and guilty for telling my mom.

In the beginning, I feared that no one would believe me because everyone thought of my brother as a fine young man. I thought that by me telling her everything the abuse would stop. I did not know how to deal with everything moving forward. I was ashamed, depressed, and my self-esteem was diminished. I did not feel comfortable in the presence of any man.

I thought of most men as a suspect. Healing can begin at many starting points and everyone's journey is different. I hoped to put it all behind me and everything would be okay, I just needed to forget it and the problem would be solved. I found myself trapped in an unhealthy connection far longer than I should have due to my mom being in denial. I still had to keep moving forward.

My brother went off to college and what a big relief that was for me. I got my bedroom which was something I was glad about. I began locking myself up in my room and I did not come out until I got hungry or needed to use the restroom. I had become completely withdrawn. I would watch cartoons all day and night.

I was determined that I was over the whole situation. Everyone overlooked it and swept it under the rug, so I was going to do the same and move forward. My mom and her boyfriend were still off and on all the time. She found out that he had a drug problem and it was hard for him to shake. Little did she know she had a problem for him also because he was hard for her to shake.

Just when I began to like him, he gave me a reason not to. My assumption of him proved to be true. He never really did anything to me, so I did not have any problem with him besides breaking out our windows all the time and me having to always leave my home due to that reason. What kind of man breaks windows? As a kid, dealing with all that chaos gave me a major problem with anxiety.

My last straw with him was when he stole the TV in my bedroom. I could not believe he took my TV clean off my dresser like I was not going to notice that it was missing. I went to school that day and came home to find my TV gone. I went and told my mom and she was like your TV is in the room. I replied, "I know I wear glasses, but I didn't see it, it's not in my room, I am certain!"

I was thinking she took my TV to punish me. She came into my room and saw that the TV was missing with her own eyes. She started searching all over the house. She blamed my second to the oldest brother, but why would he take my TV. I knew it had to be her boyfriend because he was the one home all day.

My mom went outside and began to ask the neighbors if they saw anyone walking with a TV. Our neighbor on the corner told my mom that he had seen her boyfriend walking with the TV earlier that day. I could not believe the thought; he had gone and sold my TV for a nickel rock. Why? My brothers are the ones who would try to beat him up all the time for breaking out the windows.

I however had done nothing ill towards him, so why couldn't he have taken one of their TVs? I was very perturbed. When you have an addiction problem you will do just about anything to get your fix. My brothers had told my mom the next time they saw him that they were going to mess him up. I guess my mom realized at that moment that it was best to leave him alone rather than her boys going to jail for battery/murder.

I wanted something better for my mom and he was not it, I could not do anything but empathize with her. I was determined that when I get older, I would make a better life for her and try to restore the broken mother-daughter relationship that we had. On top of that, I learned my best friend was moving away!

All I was thinking about was being left alone. I finally found a place of peace and now they were taking my place of peace from me. I was sad about them leaving but it did not really hit me until they left. I could not help it not to cry because she was more than a friend to me, she had become my sister. Her mom was like a mom, and she treated me more like her daughter. When I was over there, I ruled the house and they all treated me like the baby sister, which was how I liked it.

That is how it should have been at my home. I did not have any worries while in their care and they created a safe haven for me to come and be at peace. I spent as much time as I could in their house before they left. If I could get away with sneaking into the back of the U-Haul, I would have done just that. Her mom assured me that they would not forget about me; and any time they were in town they would be sure to come and get me.

That was when I officially became her goddaughter and she never broke that promise. I got a chance to go with them every time they came to Monroe. One thing I was learning about life was no matter what your circumstances in life are, life will continue to go on. I could not be mad at them for wanting something better and it was selfish for me to want them to stay but I felt the way I did.

My aunt and uncle moved around the corner from us due to the fact their house caught fire, so it was like when one good thing goes God will bless you with another. My mom was back to going out and dating again. The times my mom would be gone, I would just go over to my aunt and uncles' home playing with my cousins.

We all attended school together so I would just get dropped off to their house or walk around the corner to their house every day. I remember one day I was over there after school, and it was getting late. I asked my cousins to walk me home, but they did not feel like walking. I was not one to beg or plead with anyone, so I just left. I began walking up the street. I did not understand why it was almost dark and I checked the time on their computer before I had left, I forgot about daylight savings.

I took my key out of my pocket and had it in my hand ready to stick it inside the door to unlock the door. My body knows when something is not right. I was so paranoid, but I kept speed walking up the road. I was trying to hurry up and get home because I had never walked home at nighttime alone before. I was almost close to the stop sign.

I looked to my left and I saw a man walking pass Ms. Bells' yellow house. I stopped and looked back. Something told me to go back. That feeling that I get in my stomach came quickly. I looked at the man and he had made it to where my old neighbors had lived. I began walking fast to my house crossing the road. I look back and the man was jogging. I said, "O Shit!" I took off running. I looked back and the man started running full speed.

I made it to the door and put the key in and opened the door and saw him running up the driveway. I ran into the house, shut and locked the door. I heard "Blindy" while the doorknob shook. My heart sunk because there was only one person to call me that in the neighborhood. I did not get a good look at who it was because it was dark, but I was hoping it was not who I thought it was. Seconds later the horn blew. I ran to the back.

Minutes later there were knocks at the door. I heard my uncle's voice and I could have cried. I wondered if he saw the man at the door. My uncle did not like the fact that I was always left around boys and home by myself all the time. I am not sure what was about to happen, but he was my savior that night. God had a way of always protecting me.

He said, "I'm taking you back to my house. From now on your mom can come get you from the house. I am not going to have you walking at night by yourself. That was music to my ears. My uncle talked shit, he would let you know to your face and he backed up every word he spoke.

I was so thankful, but little did he know it was a little too late because it seems like the worst of the worst had already happened to me.

I knew from that point on that I would have to watch my surroundings very closely. I took a knife from the kitchen and kept a knife on me, inside of my bookbag from that moment on. I always felt safe around my uncle and aunt. It was more structured at their home than my house. They made you do chores, homework, and other things. When I was home, I did nothing but watch TV, and go outside to play if I wanted to.

At that moment, I had even considered talking to my uncle about my oldest brother, but I just did not feel comfortable telling anyone and it was embarrassing to me. I feared that he would ignore me also. The fact that he showed concern made me want to, but I just kept quiet about it and let it be.

Chapter 4
Finding Me

No worries, no problems, and no responsibilities were all the perks of being a preteen; Can you imagine that? Well, I was enjoying the moment and living life carefree. I was now in the 6th grade. I was getting older and maturing into a young lady. My body was changing more and more each day. My hips were getting wider, my breast was developing, my height was increasing, and I was gaining weight.

I was now finally wearing training bras and I got my menstrual cycle this year. I did not have to worry about my brother sexually abusing me. In fact, it is like I had forgotten about it with him being gone. So far, my school year was going great. I had made a new best friend this year and I was enjoying my 6th-grade year. My god mom and family had even moved back in the middle of the school year, which was great. On the weekends when my mom went out of town, I would be home hoping she gets back soon and majority of the time, I would stay in their house.

During the summertime, my oldest brother came home, and this put me back in depression big time. I thought that I had gotten past it and had moved on. With him being home he worked majority of the summer at Popeyes and a job at the recreation center that my mom helped him get, so I did not have to deal with him as much.

I would attend the summer program at the recreation center every year or I spend some of the summers with my dad and this year was no different. If he was gone, I was fine, but I found myself feeling hopeless and helpless now that he was back home. After building up the courage to stand up and go through with telling it solved nothing. I was still bothered by that. I didn't get it; my mom knew about the whole situation.

Now almost no one believes they would allow harmful sexual behavior to continue if they knew for sure that it was going on, right? I thought I would be protected and not harmed anymore. Here I was in the same position as before. My mom still trusted him enough to leave me alone around him. Surely, he was old enough to have a girlfriend. I was more desperate for it to stop so I began to have homicidal thoughts again.

I would often think of me taking a knife and stabbing him, but I would snap out of it quickly because that is not me and I was not going to let this situation turn me into something I am not. I tried my best to stay away from him and I kept a stand between my door making it hard for someone to even come in. After long the summer was over and he was off to school. I could not have been happier.

At this point, I was old enough to understand and I was now going to the 7th grade. I started at one school, but eventually, my mom switched me over to the Jr. high school all my brothers attended because she did not like me walking home from school alone. Now, how ironic was that? I did not know what to expect from this new school, but I was determined to make the most of it.

My young brother and I did not get along so many of them did not even know we were related unless you really knew him or me. I never talked about him and I was certain he did not talk about me. One day while in the office, the principal had got word that I was great at basketball. He said you are on the team and I want you at practice this Saturday.

I was thinking to myself, who in the hell lied. I had no skills in basketball, none whatsoever. I did not even know how to do a layup. Maybe he thought since I was the almighty little sister that I automatically knew how to play. I knew one thing for sure I was not going to make a fool out of myself, so I went home and practiced. I had only two days to get it right. I even tried praying.

I was over it and ready as I was ever going to be. I figured well; I would not make that much of a fool out of myself. When Saturday came while my mom was taking me to practice, I discovered that she was the one who told the principal that I was good at basketball and it made me angry. My mom always bragged about her kids a lot even though nothing was going right in our relationship, which I thought was backward but according to everyone, she was one proud single black mother.

She did not know everything about parenting, but she was my mom. I know she had some love for us but as a parent, she just did not know "how" was what I figured. When I made it to the gym, I dreaded getting out of the car. My stomach had knots in it and I was worried about being made fun of because the kids at this school did not let up. They would make jokes or roast you until you cried or would be ready to fight. I looked the part but unfortunately, I made a big fool out of myself. It was all worth it because I gained a group of friends.

They made fun of me not knowing how to play but I enjoyed being around each one of them some more than others. We created a bond and they were like family. Me switching schools was one of the best things going for me that school year. It was more like a sisterhood for me. One of my teammates and I became great close friends. We would always talk on the phone and write each other letters.

It was then I found out that not only did I have it bad, but her situation seemed to be worse than mine. I empathized with her and wished I could help better her situation. I learned at that very moment that I was going to try to see the bright side of things and never complain. Although I did have it bad, things could always be worse than what they are, so I learned to be grateful.

Depression makes your focus cloudy. That feeling of me not wanting to leave my room, feeling of being apathetic towards things I cared about, it was all slowly fading. No, I was never originally diagnosed with depression, but it did not take rocket science to figure it out that I was depressed. I honestly did not want to say anything about me being sad all the time because I did not want to end up in Shreveport like my second oldest brother.

I dealt with everything privately and that was the big problem. I did not trust anyone well enough to confide in them. I began to find ways to help me deal with depression. Just by being around some of the people at Carroll Jr, I started to see a whole lot of things differently. I began thinking about my life and how I wished to live it going forward.

I made a big effort to incorporate and nurture my creativity daily. I wanted a way to release some of the stressful things, so I bought myself a tablet to journal in. I began writing poems and writing everything down. This was a great help for me to express myself in a way that no one understood. I did not need anyone to talk to anymore I just wrote it down.

I even discovered that I was an excellent drawer. My friends and I would often share some of the things we drew and judge who was the best. I slowly stopped being withdrawn all the time. I would go to the mall with my friends on Saturdays or hang out at their homes if their parents were okay with it. I was beginning to be myself and I was happy about it. Taking a walk and listening to music was like an escape for me. I still had some issues to fix, I still would feel sad sometimes, and certainly needed to build my confidence up.

These were baby steps, but I was determined to be a better me. The key was to never be alone like I always was before, and I also needed a support system. Being a better version of myself is something that I always longed for. I always would daydream about my life differently and with no worries or problems. This was like an escape for me.

Although my mom was not there for me in ways I needed her to be, she was still my mom. I still did not care about all the things she had done to me in the past. She was my mom and I know you only get one mother. I was determined to love her no matter what, but it seems that the older I got the more and more resent turned into hate.

My mom did not go out during the weeks anymore, and I would still sleep in the bed with my mom even though I felt as though she did not love me, and the resentment I had towards her. My mom had started dating the dad of one of my brother's friends which in my eyes was okay because she was at home a lot more. My brother and his friends would always be over-playing the game. Everything seemed to be falling in place for me and I was happy, or so I thought.

My mom got so comfortable that she did not realize she was making a big mistake for the second time. She took to my brothers' friend – the son of the guy she dated. My mom called and treated him like her own son. I told you about that feeling I have when I know something is not right, well my gut feeling never leads me wrong.

My brother and I rode the same bus home every day. I do not know why but one day he did not ride the bus home. When the bus made it to my stop, I got up to get off. Instead of my brothers' friend going home he followed me to our house. At this point, I was much older than the times when I was a little kid, so I was not naïve. I thought to myself this boy is about to try something.

I was an analytical thinker. I told him my mom or my brother is not home so why are you coming over here? I'm about to wait for Z.B. I knew that was a lie, but I walked down the sidewalk to the house. I was scared and started to get painful knots in my stomach. When I made it to the house, I took out my key and unlocked the door.

It was normal for him to be over without my brother being home. It was practically like his home because he was at our home daily. I opened the door and went directly to my room. I took off my uniform and put on some comfortable clothes. I sat in my room and was thinking to myself, "Why do you feel like everybody is out to get you? This boy was like a practical brother to me.

I had to stop thinking that everyone was out to get me. I felt a little better so I went to the kitchen to get some frosted flakes. Walking back to my room with my cereal I saw him in my brother's room playing a game. It was a bit of relief because I had no energy to fight anymore. I was scared because I just did not feel comfortable being alone with boys, period.

Leaving me alone or evening being around boys was so uncomfortable and it made me feel as though I was naked in front of a crowd and all eyes were on me. I sat on my bed and began eating my cereal while watching Disney channel. Yes, I still watched Disney channel! After eating my cereal, I placed the bowl on top of the mirror dresser I had in my room.

I called my mom to see where she was, and I got no answer. I was starting to worry because she got off at two every day so she should have been at home. I called several times but still no answer. My brother's friend found his way to my room. I started to get the feeling of uncertainty and became nervous. He was a cool and funny dude making everyone laugh, but I put nothing past anyone because my trust was gone.

I tried to have a positive mindset and was trying not to think the worst but for some reason, I knew when I got that feeling of uncertainty that surely there was nothing good to come out of it. When he came in, he was talking to me and being his normal funny self. He began talking to me and I was being dry because I just did not feel comfortable with him being in my room. After all, we were not cool like that and when my brother or mom was around, he did not come into my room.

Shortly after coming into my room, he tried to kiss me, just like I thought. My intuition was always right. I was terrified. Where the hell was my momma? I got up trying to get out of the room, but it was like I was a piece of fresh meat to him. I wrestled with that boy trying to get him away and off me for a bit of time. I was thinking why am I always in a situation like this? It has got to be me, what am I doing to always be put in a situation like this?

He did not know what I had been through. I was tired, I had no more tears in me to cry, and my strength was completely gone. If this was God's will then I was like so be it. He was much stronger than me so I stopped wrestling with him. He removed my pants and underwear. I stared at him not moving. He got on top of me and was trying to insert his penis inside of me.

My phone rang and I picked it up quickly. "Mama where you at. You outside?" I asked, but she really said, "I'm on my way home now." My mom hung up the phone and he stood up immediately while I pretended to talk to her. He pulled his clothes back up and went back to my brothers' room. I pulled my clothes back up and softly hung up the phone.

I did not know what to think at that moment, but I was completely over everything. I had worked so hard to be a better me and get myself back out of this deep dark place that I slipped right back into it. There was no point in me saying anything because each time I would try to tell my mom, I would be dismissed quickly.

I honestly felt as though it was meant for me to be raped or something because it's like the same things keep happening like a never-ending cycle. It was like she did not know how to deal with the aftermath of it all so that was her reason for ignoring it. All those emotions came back.

I was so convinced that I had fixed this problem on my own but here I was back to those dark thoughts. This set me back. I was wondering what was wrong with me and why was everyone thinking it was okay to violate me? It had to have been me.

Atlantis's Advice:

Parents I know that sometimes you get overwhelmed with paying bills and trying to work hard to put food on the table or even wanting to have a social life of your own. No child should have to sacrifice so you can have the life you want. You don't have the right to abandon your obligation as a parent because you have other plans. You will regret it later in life. Again, your children did not ask to be here.

You are supposed to make sacrifices so that your children can have the life they deserve. To the single mothers, boyfriends and girlfriends come and go. Your kids don't. You should be eager to listen to anything your child has to tell you even if it's something small. If you cannot listen to them when they are small, then when your children grow up, they surely will not listen to you when they are grown.

You also should never leave your daughter or any girl around any boy or male. You cannot trust everyone, the main people that you think would not do any harm are the main ones you have to watch. Most of the time, it's always a relative or someone close.

Chapter 5
A Good Girl Gone Bad

For someone who has never experienced suicidal thoughts, the thought of wanting to die can make people think you are simply crazy. To them, it seems way too farfetched. If you would have known me growing up, you would have never thought I have gone through anything so detrimental like I did. I carried myself in a way that no one would even notice.

I remained that quiet and shy girl from when I was younger, but if you closely paid attention, I went from smiling all the time to always having a mug. You need your brain to do all sorts of things throughout the day but being sad made me feel nothing. I started back going into isolation and being withdrawn. Many people shy away from the conversation when it comes to a person that they may know have gone through or have taken their own life because the reality of it all is, they are frightened by it also.

The fact that a person is pretty, smart, talented, etc. can hinder the mind from becoming unwell. I did not want any attention from anyone currently. Do you know how hard it is to fight with your mind every day? The truth is I was in a serious battle with my own life. I was fighting against my thoughts, and I just could not stop overanalyzing my situation. Some may even say I am cowardly for even feeling this way.

That is why as a parent, it's important to build your children up instead of criticizing and tearing them down. The truth of the matter was I really did not want to die but I just wanted the pain I had been feeling all this time to stop. My thoughts were destroying me and were ahead in this battle. I was feeling like I was not good enough.

I continued to fight because there was nothing I could do but push forward. I was hoping things would get better. In time, I knew they would be going off how things would be going in my life; one minute I'm in a messed-up situation then the next I would be okay and happy again.

I wanted so badly to tell my mom about everything just to release all the hurt and pain that I had been feeling because it was truly damaging me, but I knew she would not have cared and I could not trust her. She showed me that all my life. So, I decided to let it go. I felt so unloved by my mom. There were no hugs, kisses, nor I love you. I was of age and my mom was not the problem anymore. I was at the age to know right from wrong, but I lacked a lot of teaching from my mom growing up.

Although I felt as though she was the cause, I could not blame her anymore. I decided that I would do what I wanted to do and not listen to anything she had to say. All at that moment everything changed. For so long I have always cared but I had a new outlook on life. In the words of "practice what you preach," well, let us just say my mom contradicted herself a lot, so I wasn't going to do a damn thing that she wanted me to do.

All my life I was good but where was it getting me? Like what the hell!!! I was tired and fed up. I was done being the nice quiet Laney from this point on I was going to raise hell. From that moment on that is exactly what I did. At school, I was normally quiet in class, but I gave the teachers hell too.

I started to get referrals and because I was on the basketball team, I would just get a paddling and would have to run extra at practice – that did not phase me though. At home, I was back to being withdrawn, so I only came out to pee and hardly had an appetite to eat anything which was not like myself.

One day my cycle was on and I went to the bathroom to use it and change my pad. I took my pad off and rolled it up and sat it on the sink next to me. I began wiping myself and I looked around me for the new pad to change, but I did not bring one in the bathroom. I placed my pad that was on the sink in the small trash can in the bathroom.

I placed tissue inside my underpants and tried to hurry back to my room to get a pad before the blood began to flow down again. I grabbed the pad and was about to head back to the bathroom and saw my mom going into the bathroom. I was thinking now she has a bathroom of her own, why on earth could she not use her own? I walked into her room and used her bathroom to put on my pad.

I threw the paper in the trash can and went back to my room. Out of nowhere, my mom started hollering and fussing. My mom began to criticize me for the pad I left in the bathroom. I'm thinking it's in the trashcan so what is the big deal? She was calling me nasty and just saying all types of mean things. It did not take much to hurt my feelings and instead of embarrassing me the way she would always do, it wouldn't hurt her if she had pulled me aside and talked to me.

I had wrapped the pad in tissue and dropped it into the trash can so I didn't understand what the problem was. I went into the bathroom just to double-check and looked to see the pad in the trashcan so I left and went to my room and did not respond. I always ignored her anyways when she fussed.

A few moments later, my youngest brother busted into my room hollering and cursing at me and told me to go get that pad out of the bathroom. My exact words to him, "I'm not doing a motherfucking thing." I don't know who the boy thought he was but I wasn't looking for a daddy and he just was out of line the way he was talking to me and it made me feel disrespected.

My brother had no problems with fighting a female and I was no different than any of the others. I knew he was going try to put his hands on me but I was not having it that day. I said, "I put the pad in the trashcan, so what is the big deal?" My mom responded, "You need to take your pads to the outside trashcan!"

To me, it just didn't make any sense because when she had her cycle exactly where did she put her pads? In the trash can in her bathroom. Why was this even a problem? I just felt like okay now they are picking. I could have complied and taken the pad out of the trash can and outside to the big trash can but I said I was not doing it. What if it was raining outside? You mean to tell me I would have to take it to the outside trashcan too? After I said, "I not going to get anything!" The boy punched me dead in the face.

I don't know what it was with my mom and me, but I felt like I was the Cinderella in the household. He walked out of my room and I walked straight to the kitchen to get a butcher knife. I was going to slice him up that day. It was like something else had taken over me. I was fed up completely with all of them. My mom saw me get the knife and walk to his room and she called the police on me.

My brother had his door closed and locked, so I started picking the lock with the knife trying to get into his room. My mom said, "I don't know what's wrong with you put that knife down. You are acting crazy." I was not trying to hear anything she had said because my brother had hit me for the last time. I picked the lock and he slammed the door quickly.

I began to punch the door with my fist letting out all my frustration while screaming. I remember picking up the knife and walking back to my room crying. I sat on the edge of my bed and dropped the knife onto the floor. I was crying like a newborn baby coming out of the womb. I just was tired of living this life. Before I could bend down to get the knife, I heard the police screaming "This is the police, put down your weapon and come out with your hands on your head."

At that moment I could not believe my mom had called the police on me. I thought to myself now I know this bitch did not call the police on me. I responded, "Y'all have to come in and kill me!!" I slid the knife up under my bed. I heard them walking in the hallway towards my door and I knew they would have a gun pointed at me and I did not care if they shot me.

I was tired of being in the situation. I felt hopeless. All my life I was at a battle and to say I made it this far I would say I was a strong soldier. The light was off in my bedroom and I saw a flashlight shadow from under my door. I heard one knock and then the door bust open. It was a black cop that came in with all that unnecessary hollering. I said, "Damn!" While turning my head sideways giving him a mug.

I did not have the weapon in my hand, and I was sitting there still. The police grabbed me and threw me on the ground. I told him all this is unnecessary; you do not even have to do all that. He responded, "You trying to be a badass is also unnecessary. Exactly, how am I trying to be a badass? I told him just because you were picked on in school doesn't give you the right to abuse your badge pussy!"

The police picked me up and slammed me back on the ground knocking almost every bit of wind left in me out making my forehead hit our ceramic tile floor. I did not say another word because Mr. officer was really showing out. I was in a difficult situation and he had the upper hand. He put the handcuff on my hands picked me up and walked me out. All I could think was why does my mother hate me so much?

I said to myself man I hate this lady! I looked straight ahead going out of the house. The black officer stopped and said, "Apologize, now!" For me disrespecting my mom. I did not have one word to say but you can take me to jail. I felt like I was not being disrespectful because they just did not know all the traumatic experiences I have dealt with. I was nervous about going but I felt a bit of relief not having to deal with all their craziness.

The white officer must have had some sympathy for me because he said, "I got her and walked me to his police car and put me in. The handcuffs were so tight I could not feel my hands. He loosened them up before closing my door. Thank you I replied. We sat there for a couple of minutes and I looked and saw the black officer talking to my mom.

Tears began to fill my eyes. I closed them tightly but that did not stop them from flowing. The officer began to drive off and green oaks was an opposite way from the way he was going and I was thinking where is he taking me? At that moment, I started to over-analyze the situation and thought that the worst was about to happen. I just did not say anything and was ready for whatever that was going to happen.

The white officer tried to make small talk, but I did not have anything else to say to anyone. I kept my head down and would just look out the corner of my eye because I just felt like I was not wrong. I did not want the officer to see me crying and think that I was soft. Some may say I caused the problem but to me that was me trying to release out all my frustration that had been building up for so many years.

I was tired and, at that point, I knew that I went overboard. I thought to myself, acting out was not helping the situation either, but at that moment, I did not care. The resentment I had for her was so deep.

While in that car, the police officer said, "I know you're listening even if you don't respond! Don't you ever get to the point where you are so angry that you want to pull a knife and stab someone. It's easy getting into trouble but hard to get out of it. Next time I want you to find a better way to let your anger out. I don't want to have to come back to your house."

I knew that was God speaking through him to me, so instead, I replied you're right okay." Because I knew for every choice that is made there is a consequence. I was not using my brain. I will never forget the words that he spoke to me. When we made it to the juvenile detention center, he said promise me that this is your first and last time coming to this place. I looked at him sideways and responded, I do not make promises because a promise can be broken, so that means I would be standing up here lying to you dead in your face.

I am a woman of my word so the only thing I can tell you is I will try." He smiled and said, "Wow! Any other kid would have told me a lie right to my face. A woman? I appreciate your honesty. A kid like you does not belong in a place like this. I can see that you are not that type of young lady. I see you are wise beyond your years, so I know that you are smart enough to find a better choice in the way you release your anger. You're human and it's okay that you made a mistake but learn from it!"

The officer was right. I guess he was trying to lighten the situation and make me feel a little better. He did make me feel better. I had a lot to deal with and it was a lot to deal with for me. I never thought of a way of releasing the anger I had built up inside. I was now calmer and back to thinking normally. I was wrong for the choice that I made, I felt bad. I could not understand; why does it take other people to talk to me and I could not even get that type of care and concern from my own mom.

I should have handled it better, but it was no turning back. I was already in handcuffs being walked into intake so I could not take any of it back. I was ready to go to my cell and be off to myself, just the way I preferred. After they processed me in, I went straight to my cell. I did not get a meal or anything. They made me tote my mattress and the jumpsuit was too little, but I did not say one word. They told me the rules and put me in my cell.

The next morning, I was awakened at five in the morning. I just knew these people were not serious. I was asleep and my hand was aching from me punching the door. I had to make up the bed, brush my teeth, and come out to eat breakfast. The food was delicious, and not like slop like I always heard. I was so uncomfortable being in juvie with my period on.

You can call me crazy. I thought jail would be the worst place ever, but I did not actually mind being in there. It was just like home if you asked me. Just that I could not watch TV like I would do all day every day and you were around immature girls. I had to go to school also while I was there and I got a chance to see a counselor which I think was a great and much needed experience.

Our talk was very heartfelt and she helped to open my eyes about a lot. After making it back from seeing the counselor I was told I had to go to my cell. I was in there maybe thirty minutes and one of the guards came to my cell and told me I had a visitor. I was like a visitor? When

I made it to the visitation room, I saw my mother sitting on the other side of the glass. I did not even sit down, I backed up and walked away.

The guard said where are you going? I looked at her sided eye and said, "Back to my cell I don't want to talk to her; she's the reason I'm in here so what are we going to talk about?" The older guard came and got me and said baby please go and talk to your mom. I hardly ever see parents coming to see their kids and some have been in here months and you've only been in here a day; she must really care about you."

Tuh! Or better yet the guilt is getting at her, I replied. "Do it for me?" asked the guard. My stubbornness had got the best of me. I looked at her and said to myself I do not even know you all that well to be doing favors. I just got up and walked back around to the visitation room. I sat down and picked up the phone and said, "What do you want?" My mom replied.

"You need to stop acting crazy." If you came up here to talk about me acting crazy then you are wasting your time. You're the reason I am half crazy! I don't know why you came to see me because this is where I am better off anyway. I am the problem and a nonfactor to you. The only reason you came up here is that you feel bad about calling the police when you should not have even called them in the first place.

I don't need you coming up here seeing me or worrying about me. You weren't worried about me all these years so don't start doing it now!" I hung up the phone and got up and walked back to my cell. I knew I was being harsh and said some hateful things, but I was angry. The times I needed her she was never there and would always dismiss me so I decided to give her a taste of her own medicine.

I felt bad for saying everything I said, and I wanted to apologize but she never apologized for the hurtful things she said to me. I just had this *"it was what it was"* type of attitude. While in my cell with no TV to watch I had a lot to think about. When it was dinner time, the guards were getting ready to do a shift change.

The younger guard came up to me and said, "Are you calm?" I replied, "I'm always calm." She said baby listen, I don't know you nor do I know your situation. The way you talked to your mom was very disrespectful and I did not like it. My mother is dead and seeing the way you talked to your mom, I could not believe it. Kids are in for months and you were only in here a day, and your mom came up here.

"My mom doesn't love or care about me?" I replied. When you got up, I picked up and apologized on your behalf. You talked so harshly that she began to cry." Now I had never seen my mom cry, so I just figured she probably was making it up. "And she told me to tell you she loves you!" replied the guard. I had not recalled my mom ever telling me she loved me and just the thought made me burst into tears.

The lady did not even understand my reasoning for saying all of what I said but she was right I should not have said it at all. I know that you only get one mother and you should cherish her while she was here on earth but at this point, I was honestly satisfied with hurting her as much as she had hurt me. If something was to happen to her I was prepared to live with knowing I said all those mean and hurtful things to her.

Another choice I made and would have to live with. I was an emotional roller coaster. All that night I was thinking what if something happens to my mom. The words replayed back in my head. I did not get any rest, crying majority of the whole night and the rock I was sleeping on was so uncomfortable.

When that Monday arrived, it was time for me to go to court. In court, I was so nervous that I had bad gas. Was I going to be sentenced and given time like those other girls? Juvie was cool but I did not want to be in there for six months like the others. It was not like I had stabbed anyone and then the police did not even see the knife, they just went off based on whatever my mom told them.

Even though I acted as if I did not care, I really wanted to go home and be with my mom. I plead guilty to all the charges. The judge had his saying and I was not listening because my mind was cluttered. I was put on probation and had to go to anger management classes. I was a bit relieved because I would not have to stay but I was dreading going back home to my mom and my brother whom I hated because I would have to act like I was still mad at them.

I had to go back to my cell. Maybe an hour later we got a chance to go outside to play ball, but I did not stay long because my mom had arrived. I had to go and clean out my cell and give them back the mattress and other things. I was given back my clothes and they processed me out and released me back to my mom. I was still putting on that "I don't give a fuck" attitude.

I got in the back seat and did not say one word to her the whole ride home. When I made it to the house I just went to my room and closed the door. My mom would try to talk to me, but I was not giving in because I had no words for her.

It was like she felt bad but at the end of the day, she ignored me majority of my 12 years being on this earth now suddenly you care. I was just done, and I knew I was wrong for the way I disrespected her but whatever the consequences were, I was just going to have to deal with that on my own.

After being back home, I would just be in my room all day most of the time crying. I began to reflect on my life and I began to think that maybe I'm the problem. I began to think that maybe everyone would be better without me. My vision was becoming blurred again with that dark cloud falling back into that old pattern.

I was not eating because I did not have an appetite. I just decided that I did not want to be bothered with any of them. The best way to not get your heart broken, is to pretend you do not have one. You cannot make anyone love you. The struggle I was having to heal myself and cope was a mighty one. I had let all these emotions build up and one thing I wish more people would understand is feeling numb. I was not sad anymore, nor could I cry or feel sorry for myself.

At that point, I felt nothing. I was back to being withdrawn in my room all day sleeping my life away. At school, if someone picked on me, I did not even react at all. If teachers would talk to me, I was not hearing nor processing anything. I was not being my normal goofy self. I was experiencing more anxiety and I would even sometimes have panic attacks. I was completely emotionless.

I started skipping class, smoking cigarettes and weed with the girl at my school who I later found out we were related. I even started self-medicating myself heavy taking my mom's Lortab's just so I would not feel anything. I even would take the knife that I kept on me and began cutting myself. I still felt nothing. I just was ready to end it all.

The thoughts of my past were really attacking me, but God sent me an angel to get me back going in the right direction. Do you believe in angels? God was always right on time in my life. I was falling so deep in despair, but God sent me an angel to show that I was loved and cared for and he was with me every step of the way and little did I know that the journey for my life was much harder than others because the calling he had for my life was much higher. Everything was part of the plan he had for my life. Instead of me trusting him, I began to drown myself deep in my circumstances and the world around me.

Atlantis's Advice:

You are responsible for your actions no matter how you feel or no matter the situation. Anger never solves the problem, but it does destroy everything. Being angry only brings out the worst and the best thing you can do is learn is how to contain yourself when upset. Holding in everything never solves the problem either.

Also, if you are ever in a situation where you feel as though your mom does not love you or you are not loved, it does not give you the right to be disrespectful to anyone. Your mother is your mother and you only get one. Your mom cannot be replaced, nobody can do what your mom does, and no one can compare to your mom.

Mothers are human and they make mistakes just like us, but it is all a learning experience. Your mom's negative behavior can be toxic to you. For so long my mom treated me in a way that it made me doubt if I was important to her, (my worth) and that I was not deserving of love, approval, and validation. Know that only God can love you more than she does.

No matter what your mom has done to you, you will be sorry when she is gone. Again, you are not responsible for what others do but you are responsible for you. Mothers that have not truly healed the hurt they have been through tend to hurt their daughters. When you do not feel good about yourself, you act in ways that hurt others and it may not even be intentional but only because you are hurting. In any situation always think about the consequences before acting. Own your anger and learn to be in control of you.

Chapter 6
Earth Angel

Just when I thought there was no choice but to cease all motion and give into what seemed like an unbeatable nightmare, I met an earth angel. She was not an angel sent down on earth. This angel I met was disguised as an ordinary person and had been here for years.

At first, she had this demeanor that came off as this mean and rude lady but the more and more I was in her presence I was surrounded by warmth, care, and she was a concerned person. She believed in going out of her way to help others, she did not like a mess and always diffused conflict. She wanted everyone to be happy and even though she did not play, she was about her business.

This lady believed in me and she taught me to stand up and believe in myself. I would miss the bus on purpose just to go over to the rec and be around her. When I was there, I would laugh and play with my friends, but I really would come just to be around her. Majority of the time she would sit outside in front of the rec and smoke her cigarettes.

She had a mouthpiece on her and would be talking mad shit. I would be so tickled at her, but she would mainly just be having fun. I enjoyed going to the rec, but she was just so mean. My mom would come and pick me up from the rec almost every day. She would be upset because she knew I was not missing the bus that much.

One day they ended up talking and she told my mom I want you to leave her up here with me, stop sending her home by herself. Finally, someone understood the importance of not leaving a young girl at home alone. I was thinking why does she even care but learned that it was just in her nature to care and help all.

Every day I looked forward to getting up and going to that rec and being up under her all the time. I was no longer in that dark space at all. She had grandchildren and her granddaughter (that was my age) and I also became close friends. One rainy day, I was alone with her in the office and she was on the phone talking. She asked me to help her straighten some of the papers that scattered everywhere in her office, and I was glad to help; anything she would ask me to do I was ready.

I was straightening and getting rid of papers and she stopped out of nowhere and said, "Bye I got to go!" She slammed the phone down and said, "Go to the kitchen." I was confused but I did exactly what she asked me to do without asking any questions. She hurt my feelings hollering at me, I did not know what I did.

I did not like people hollering at me, so it made me get in my feelings big time. I jumped up on the counter and began talking to myself. "I don't know who this lady think she is, she's not my momma. I don't even let my momma holler at me. This will be my last day coming up here, watch!" When she came into the kitchen she closed and locked the door. She still had the cordless phone in her hand.

She walked up to me and pointed the cordless phone directly in my face and said, "What the hell is wrong with you? I moved my head back; I was baffled, and I thought to myself this lady is fucking crazy, what did I do? I replied nothing is wrong with me." She grabbed my arm and said, "It got to be something wrong with your ass because you are cutting yourself.

Pulling on the bandage wrap I had over my wrist. I looked at my arm and noticed that the wrap I had on my arm was pushed up. I honestly did not realize that it had even moved. It must have moved up with all that moving I was doing when I was helping to clean up her office. I would lie and tell people at school that my hand got jammed and that was my reason for wearing it.

She said, "Nothing should ever be that bad to the point where you are self-harming yourself. Talk to me and tell me what is wrong" I was speechless and did not know what to say. I just broke down crying like a baby. I did not trust anyone, and I did not really want to say anything but I knew if I didn't say anything, she would probably tell my mom.

I did not like my mom in my business because I could not trust her, she felt it was okay to tell family members or her friends my business. A lot of people would say I am sneaky or secretive and that I needed to be watched. Honestly, all my life, people showed me that you cannot trust anyone and the only person I could rely on was myself. If you got a chance to know me, you would learn that I was not a sneaky or mischievous person.

I was a trustworthy person; I never was one to run off at the mouth with no one's personal information and I was hoping that I could get the same in return from her. I asked her to promise not to say anything because I did not want anybody knowing my business because I was embarrassed and felt ashamed about it, and I learn to keep my life private.

I told her everything that happened to me starting from the time when I was with my mom at her friend's house until that point that I had ever experienced. She hugged me so tightly for the longest and she began to cry with me. At that moment I knew she had to be sent by God in my path. She did not judge me or talk bad about me.

I was thinking; if I had stayed at the other school; I would not have even met her. It's so crazy how God works I thought! This was God and I felt it right at that point. At this age, I had my doubts about God and every time I got into a situation, things would always happen and work out in my favor. I did not want to even go to another school, but it had to happen, and it was so amazing to me.

She empathized with me, encouraged and even prayed with me. Before we left the kitchen, she said to me; "You have a purpose in your life. What you have been through will be used for the glory of God. "While you are up here with me, I assure you that you will not have to worry about being hurt or harmed and I promise not to tell anyone about what you told me.

I will take it to the grave, smiling at me. Promise me you will not do that crazy ass shit anymore? "she said. I said chuckling, "I'm not. I was just in a dark place and feeling as though it was a way to end all my pain!" She told me to stop having that victim mentality. You must forgive and let go. You are self-sabotaging yourself and drowning yourself in your sorrow, it is not the way.

Baby, you are not your circumstances. You got to keep moving. Life is not easy; some people have it better than others that is just how it is. God gave you a different journey than most because you are strong enough to go through it. I wiped my tears and hugged her tightly. She chuckled and said now go to the bathroom and get yourself together.

Go now with your crazy ass!" I smiled from ear to ear. Damn, I love this lady, I thought to myself. I thanked God because Lord knows she came into my life at the right moment. It is all according to God's will. The word forgiveness stayed in my head. She was right I had to forgive. Right there, I decided that I would forgive my mom, the evil man, my brother, brothers' friend and everyone else that had done something wrong to me; stop bringing up the past.

I felt so relieved to get all that pain that I had been harboring inside me out for the first time. I was now going to move forward and let that be. I did not miss a day at the rec from that day forward. I enjoyed being the rec baby as they called me. I learned to play cards, dominos, and pool with the old men that came up there every day. The rec had become a haven for me. I was feeling myself at this point and my confidence began to build up. I started caring for myself a lot more.

I met my middle school lover around this time.

The first day of my 8th grade school year was lovely. I was still on the basketball team and I ended up taking the same teacher my brother had when I was in the 7th grade. She was loud and extra, but she was like a mother figure to me and I loved her just as much. Upon meeting him, I was conversing with someone who I was falling for. I ended up talking to him through a mutual friend from school.

Last school year, we had a couple of classes together but this year we did not have any together so I would always see him on the way to other classes. He would always make me smile and blush. I honestly did not expect to be in a relationship with him, but he was someone I enjoyed conversing with on the phone in the beginning.

Whether I like it or not, he found a way to integrate himself into my life. I was forced with the option of choosing between him and the person I had feelings for. I welcomed seeing him every day at school and I was quite sure he did not know it. The more and more I talked to him, the more things I found out we had in common. He was born in February and so was I; our birthdays were two days apart.

His mom was born in February and so was my mom and the crazy part of it is that they were born on the same day. We would be on the phone much of the night until his mom would bust into the room and make him get off, which I thought was funny because based on the image he portrayed, you would not think his mom cared.

It was not long before we became boyfriend and girlfriend. I was thinking since we were both Pisces, we would share a lot in common, but he was truly the opposite of myself. I began thinking he is not a Pisces, or he has to be a different breed of it. He would put on this thug boy act trying to be somebody he was not, but I was no one to judge so I liked him for who he was and tried to focus on the positives.

We would talk about any and everything. I got so comfortable talking to him that I shared with him some of the things I had endured throughout my childhood. He assured me that he had my back and did not have to worry about any of that while we were dating. One day before school, my brother and I got into an altercation. Which was always because we never got along, and he thought he was so hard.

I pushed him making him hit his head on the door and the boy turned around and punched me dead in my eye. My glasses broke making a cut and bruise under my eye. I told my boyfriend about it and he said, "Don't worry I'm going to beat his ass." The next day when he saw my eye he was heated. It was not really all that bad, but it was a bruise under my eye.

When his cousin saw my eye, he said, "son we're going to get that nigga together. What kind of nigga put his hands on a female and your sister at that? Don't worry lil' cuz we're going to get that nigga for you!!!" Man, I was so happy. I wanted them to beat my brother's ass because he got on my nerves and he thought he was so hard. Funny thing is my brother ended up getting checked out of school that day.

I love the fact that he was being protective of me; I was not used to it. That made me feel good to know that someone cared about me. It is supposed to be a natural thing to want to protect the one you love from harm, heartbreak, or unhappiness and this gave me great comfort. On Saturdays, we would meet up at the mall, movies, or find somewhere to hang out. We enjoyed our first year together and looked forward to going to high school together.

That summer we got into a serious romantic relationship which was a major development milestone for me. Going into high school we were still together. My favorite teacher told me you will get married just like her co heart at the school. I didn't see it, but I did idolize the type of relationship my aunt and uncle had because they met in the eighth grade and was together ever since. I wanted a forever love like theirs.

Somethings I longed for was to find someone to love me flaws and all; I wanted to be like my aunt and uncle. We shared a close bond and I got to see a side of him that no one else got to see. I even developed a close bond with his mom, and she would always say you are the daughter I never had. It was nice to know that I had people to call on now and that was in my corner.

His mom would do things for me that she did not do for him and this made him kind of jealous; however, it made me love her so much more than my mom. During our first year of high school, our relationship started having emotional ups and downs. When you are around a person for a long time, their true character will begin to show.

He displayed anger issues all the time lashing out at people, but I would always try to keep his head on the right track. I felt like I owed him since he would always be so protective, loving, and caring of me. It was not long before he began lashing out at me also. Having a protective boyfriend is a good thing, but there is a big difference between protective and possessive.

It is also completely natural to want to protect your relationship, warding off potential matches. We were known in high school so you had the seniors that would prey on the "Fresh(meat)men" girls. If you value someone, you do not want to lose them and that is supposed to be the root of protectiveness. To some, the difference is obvious, but there are many overlapping grey areas between the two.

Now to me, protectiveness requires trust, while possessiveness requires doubt. Rather than love and devotion, he was always running off negative emotions all the time and from experience, this is something that I really did not need in my life. To me, I knew that he was young, but he was very immature in the mind. I know I was insecure about my worth and I never had anyone telling me or guiding me properly while growing up.

Before I knew it, he began to put me down to make himself feel good. He would take my phone and go through it like I was just a big hoe and I was not even talking to anyone but him. This was all because he was the one being conniving. Then he would flip the switch and say I love you and I do not want you to leave me. I would be thinking to myself, where exactly I am going with this boy?

Shit, he was beginning to drain my soul. He did not want me hanging around some of my classmates that I would talk to nor did he want me talking to other guys which I could understand to a certain extent. He always showed concern for my safety when it came to certain decisions, but this is undoubtedly a controlling behavior.

When we would get into an argument, he would put his hands on me and this was coming from the same boy that was angry with my brother for always fighting me. Afterward, he would always become apologetic and would revert to how his dad put his hands on his mom as a child. I guess this made it right for him to put his hands on me.

I always thought what you endured as a child should make you want to be or do better. He would always get upset about me talking to other people at school, but he was the main one cheating. People would always try to come and tell me this or that, but I did not care what anyone had to say because I was going to do what I wanted to do. If I did not see anything with my own eyes, then I was okay because some of them were liars and did not want to see you in a happy relationship because they could not keep a man. In my mind, I felt like I was winning.

Honestly, I knew this was not what I wanted but I was hoping he would revert to the original guy I met in the beginning. Anything he did, I would reciprocate the same thing that was done to a certain extent. In other words, it is no fun when the rabbit got the gun! He began saying I would always be nagging, tripping, or being difficult. I am being difficult because my feelings were essential? It was like he wanted someone he could get over on and I was not her, so I decided to leave him alone and let him be.

The summer my mom found out that I had sex with him, she wanted me to go with my oldest brother "the pervert" and his girlfriend and daughter. Exactly, how was this supposed to help the situation? I have no idea, but this put me back into depression big time! I really was not for him trying anything but now that he had a girlfriend, he had not tried anything with me, and boy I was happy.

I loved visiting Baton Rouge because my favorite rapper was from there, but I was not looking forward to going to stay with my brother for an entire summer. It was like she wanted me out of her hair because she now had a boyfriend that lived with us and I hated him. He was no good, and I saw right through him, but I did not say anything. I just had to make the most of my situation because there was honestly nothing I could do.

That summer was depressing and the first day I was down there, my brother and his girlfriend left their daughter and I at her great grandma's house. I remember the lady waking us up for church the next morning. I got up brushed my teeth, did my hair, put on my clothes, and waited in the room to leave with them for church. I was listening to my iPod and I was kind of hungry.

I got up and went into the living room looking for the lady to ask if it was okay I got something to eat but she was not there. I went into her den and there was no one in the den and the lights were off. The lady took her granddaughter and left without me for church. I was pissed off. There was nothing in there for me to eat, so I was starved out.

I called my mom and told her I wanted to come home. Instead, she called my brother's girlfriend who came and got us.

I was depressed about the breakup between my ex and I, so I decided to call and try to confide in my mom about my feelings. I called her and told her how I was feeling but she had no advice for me or any form of sympathy – what a waste. I knew that was a big mistake, but I called her anyway, and not only was she not of any help, she told my business to my brother and this came up in an argument later.

I said, "Never again will I ever try to talk to this lady." I didn't know what I was thinking about and this is where my trust issues came about in the first place. While down there, my brother did not do anything to me, but I could not help but wonder about the little girl. I noticed how he walked around in his underwear and she would often be in the room when he was getting ready for work. This did not sit well with my spirit.

I did not say anything the first time, but I was hoping he did not do anything to her because I was the same age she was when the abusing started with me. One day I took her for a walk to the gas station to get us some snacks, this was my way of getting her alone to talk to her about somethings.

I talked to her about boys and I also discussed to her that she shouldn't be going into a room with a grown man while they are getting dressed because men are not like women, and their body parts are different. I also wanted to bring up the situation about my brother but I didn't because she had a love for him and I didn't want to kill her spirit with what happened to me so I kept quiet.

It didn't seem like he had done anything to her and she was more different than me so I decided to just make a different conversation because it was making me depressed and I didn't want to even think about it. I like being around his girlfriend because she would take me to the stores and we would go shopping all the time.

I enjoyed conversing with her but I missed home and was ready to get back to my bed because I would sleep on the floor down there and it was so uncomfortable. I did not come back home until it was time for school to start. My summer down there was not that bad, and I was hoping I ran into my favorite rapper every time we went somewhere.

I was glad to be back home. I missed the rec and all my friends. My 10th-grade year was okay, but I learned towards the end of the year that the lady at the rec had to leave and go home for a while because she had cancer. I was hoping things were just temporary. My ex and I ended up back together that year. We shared good and some bad experiences that year.

During my 11th grade year, the boy gave me hell. A lot of people would always tell me that you can do better, and you do not need to be with someone like him. A lot of people would say I would never put up with that and I often say I would never do that but, at that moment, I learned you should never say "Never." I found myself in a lot of situations where I was doing exactly what I said I would never do! Nothing is impossible and anything can happen.

I knew they were right but here I was trying to stay down and just remain my true loyal self and I was not the type of girl to hop from person to person. I was thinking he is young right now he will get himself together. The truth of the matter is I was stuck and feeling regretful because I choose to be with him over the person I really wanted to be with.

I was heartbroken and was dealing with that at the time and my boyfriend started talking to one of the girls in school. We ended up breaking up that year because of him cheating. He would always deny it, but I was not crazy. He must have forgotten I had three brothers. I saw all the stupid lies they told girls, tricks, and games they along with their friends played.

I would often think damn they are dumb putting up with that type of foolishness but here I was being foolish myself. I was not about to let him run those types of games on me. He was trying to talk to me and the other girl at the same time. I was so over him and decided to break it off with him. The boy was still trying to talk to me but I was hearing about everything that he had going on.

I never discussed anything with him but if he wanted her, then I was going to let him do so because I was not about to let him try to make a fool out of me. It was just the fact of him embarrassing and shaming me. People got a pleasure off of seeing others hurt, but this was because they weren't happy with themselves.

Here I was being this good and loyal girlfriend to hear from others that I am really being played and looked like a fool, that is truly a hurtful experience. I was used to not talking about my problems and acting as if everything was okay. On the other hand, I was deeply upset, so acting as if nothing was happening and not talking about it was my way of dealing with it.

Many people would say I thought I was better but I never thought I was better than anyone. Little did they know I went through more things than anyone. My trust was ruined at an early age so many things that I experienced in my childhood shaped me into the person I was later in my teen and even adult years. I would be calling him out on everything. One day at school, we were in the stairway talking and I remember telling him okay, if you're not talking to this girl then let's go and ask her.

Seeing the girl in the stairway, I was going to ask her and this boy said leave her alone Laney man I am not about to let you fight that girl. This really had pissed me off because he confirmed what I already knew at that moment; he was playing both sides. I began to build up anger toward him because I had never really done anything foul or wrong towards him for him to treat me the way he was trying to treat me.

I did not understand how he could even treat me like that, and I always had his back. No one could tell me anything because I honestly already knew this boy had no loyalty to me at all. I felt like if you're going to treat me like this over a girl and claim to genuinely love me then just go ahead. I decided to let him go and just deal with the hurt. I was completely done.

I remember talking to his mom about the situation and she even denied him talking to someone else and he had this lady completely fooled. In fact, the way he treated her was no better than how he treated me and I should've known if he had no respect and could lie to his mom all the time the way he did, what on earth made me any different? I started to move on with my life.

He would still be trying to talk to me, but it was over for me. I started to go to parties and have fun. I did not really get a chance to enjoy myself due to him not wanting me to go places or do things and it was okay because I was used to being in the house and stuff most of the time anyway. I still was hurt about the situation.

One day I was walking down the hall by the cafeteria about to go to Ms. Fleming's class. The girl was on the opposite side of the hallway and magically appeared when I looked back up on the side I was on. She was with her friends and had bumped into me. At first, I remember being like okay I'm just going to let her go on because I'm not about to have people thinking I want to fight over a nigga. After all, he definitely wasn't worth all of that.

I am a junior and she was a freshman, let it go. All these thoughts began to pop up in my head and I really felt played, so I remember making a U-turn and was like fuck it. I began looking for her but somehow, she managed to go to the office. The police in the school came to me and said "why are you trying to fight her over a boy that ain't shit?" I was confused because I was not talking to him in school, on the phone, or through any other means.

Her brother came up to me and said chill out Atlantis. Just found out that the boy had gone to tell them that I was trying to fight the girl over him. This really pissed me off, so I had something for both of them. I had put up with a lot of his shit and truly the girl did not owe me anything but anger consumed me and I acted without thinking. I went to the office and jump over the secretary's desk and started punching her in the head.

The principal and assistant principal tried to pull us apart, but we both fell to the ground and she kicked me in the stomach and I smacked her dead in the face. The assistant principal took her into his office. I was mad as hell. The police came in there and said, "See now you're stubborn as hell and don't listen. I'm taking you to jail."

He walked me through the principal's office out his side door and I saw my ex standing there looking like a sad puppy. I ran away from the police and ran up towards him and spit in his face. The police said, "You too quick for me. Now was that worth it?" I said, "Naw because you ain't give me the opportunity to fuck him up!" He laughed and said, "You know you really had me fooled because I did not know you could act like that!

As pretty and quiet as you are, I thought differently." He asked me how old I was, and I was only sixteen, so I had to go back to juvie. On the ride there, I remember thinking okay you really did not have to do all that. It was like I was causing my storms. Honestly, I felt bad for the way I acted. I was older than the girl and should have taken the higher road, but I let those negative thoughts overpower the positive ones.

Oh well because for every choice there is a consequence and this was mine, so I had to deal with it. I was just fed up with a lot. After they processed me in, I walked to the back and sat down at the table and began playing checkers with one of the girls at the table. Later, I got a call from my mom, and I was talking to her and she said I have somebody who wants to talk to you." It was my ex.

I said mama hang this boy up I do not want to talk to him, I am trying to get out of here. He was so regretful and trying to explain but

I was not trying to hear a damn thing he had to say because I really wanted to cut his ass up with my knife. I knew that he was only trying to talk to me because things did not work out as he had planned.

He was talking and I just held the phone away from my ear for a couple of seconds then I put it back to my ear and said I had to go and hung up the phone. I did not want to hear that bull shit. I was getting disgusted and was fed up with him. Once I got out, I was on suspension and could not go to school for three days. My ex was blowing me up trying to talk and everything.

I decided to ignore him because it truly had hurt me and I just knew that was not real love. When Valentine's day came, he showed up with a bear, shoes, clothes, jacket, jewelry. He was trying to win me back. He lost my trust and everything. I was still pissed off about how he treated me.

I got wind that the lady from the rec was not doing too well. My last time ever seeing her was at the benefit they had at the recreation center for her and I was in tears seeing how little she had got and knowing things were not going to get any better for her. It reminded me of my favorite aunt on my dad's side that passed away because the last time I saw her was at the benefit that they had for her at the church in St. Joe. Shortly after she had died.

It was hard for me to see her like that. I mean she was skinny, but she had gotten super skinny. I went by to see her and she was at her moms' house one time and upon leaving, all I could do was cry. Now the thought of losing her was truly going to break my heart. I did not know when but I knew God was going to take my angel away. In March she died, and I remember feeling nothing. The lady that loved me as if I were her own was gone.

I remember going into my room crying silently and I felt numb again. I punched myself in the head and kicked my legs as if I were a toddler throwing a temper tantrum. I was stronger enough than before to deal with it and not like the other times where the dark cloud was coming back into my vision. That lady truly built me up. I remember texting her granddaughter trying to say some encouraging words.

I missed half the funeral because I was not a funeral type of person. I had made it far because of that lady; what was I going to do without her. The rec was not the same and I stopped going. I leaned more towards my ex for comfort and started back conversing with him. I remember him talking about us being back together and how he was going to do better and selling me a bunch of dreams again and I fell for it.

In my senior year of high school, I remember thinking this is my year and I am going to make the most of it and have me some fun. I did just that and I even started my first job. I was doing well for myself. I was proud of the progress I made so far and was now heading in the right direction. I graduated and decided to start my college journey at Southern University.

My mom did not really want me to go off to college at southern, but I honestly liked the school because of the times I visited when my mom took my older brother back to school and because it was a HBCU. I wanted to be far away from home. I wanted to come out and be my natural self. I need a new setting and really wanted to start over. I like the fact that she was showing a bit of concern.

I thought about who would I have to lean on besides my older brother and that was no option for me; so I decided to go to Grambling or ULM, but my boyfriend didn't want me to go to either because he didn't want me to go far away from him but I honestly felt that he didn't want me to get around them fine college boys and I would leave his ass. He never said it but I knew that's what it was, so I decided to settle for ULM.

I got my classes set up and I was ready to go. When school began, the people in the registrar's office told me that I would have to start next semester due to the fact I had a low score on my ACT. I did not understand why they waited until school to tell me that, so I decided to go to Delta Community College.

I was working and going to school. I knew exactly what I wanted for myself or so I thought. I was determined to become a registered nurse because they got paid big money. I loved caring for people and it was one of my true passions. Trying to maintain a job to pay for the bills I had and study at the same time was becoming a bit much.

I was trying to help my mom with bills and save up for a car to get myself back and forth to school. My grandma was taking me to school and work almost every day, and I knew that was a lot of wear and tear on her and her vehicle. I knew that she was probably tired, so I took on an extra job. I was trying to push my boyfriend to do something with himself instead of roaming the streets all day. That was also strenuous on me, and while I was trying to be productive, he was back to his same ways.

I was starting to see that he was not maturing and he honestly did not know what he wanted. I empathized and I was determined to help him do better for himself. I was goal orientated and when it came to my future after all the hell I endured; I was determined to come out on top; I also wanted the same for him. Love is blind and I mean literally! He did wrong things and I was not an angel too. My problem was I did not mind giving him a second chance.

This was one of my many flaws; I literally had a list of personality traits and flaws that proved he was never deserving of a girl like me. I overlooked a lot and I decided to love him despite all the bad. I accepted the fact that he wasn't perfect. He hurt me, disappointed and upset me a lot. I had a good heart, I was caring, loyal, and no matter what I remain true.

The truth of the matter is that no matter how good you are as a woman, you will never be good enough for someone who is not ready. I prayed about it and I asked God to reveal to me the truth and what I needed to do. After a while, I was honestly over him and I ended up finding out that he had a secret Facebook page that I did not know about.

He was trying to talk to other girls and was just making me look like a fool, yet again. I was the type of girl that had FBI credentials and you really could not hide anything from me. There it was – my confirmation. I decided I was done with this boy once again. I remember wanting to know why? Why treat me like this? This boy had known almost everything about me and what I have been through.

He started off loving and portraying himself to be the perfect guy, but it was all an act if you ask me. I had realized who this boy was and he was not the one. I didn't trust him at all because he ruined that already and my trust doesn't come with a refill. Once it's gone it's gone. I was hoping that he could try to restore it, but it still was not the same for me. I had to stop and think, what exactly is this boy helping me to accomplish? How is he motivating me? What exactly was he doing to help me become a better me? Not a motherfucking thing! For me, it was over and I was done with him and this time I meant it for good. I said if God wanted me with him then it would not be this hard and draining so I decided to leave him alone.

My emotions were all over the place and the dark cloud that always comes into my vision was coming back my way. I would be crying all the time. I was getting back depressed. At work, it was hard trying to remain my happy self as people thought. I was truly unhappy with myself and was feeling a bit lost. I would always pray and ask God for guidance. I went to church every Sunday and sometimes I would often just sit there drowning in my tears.

Lord knows I did not want to slip back into my old ways but here I was going back. To everyone, I appeared perfectly happy but deep down I was back living with depression. I remember working late one night at the service desk. My body was feeling weird and to be honest, I thought it was just me because my period came on late. I was so emotional when my cycle came on that you would think I'm bipolar.

I remember talking to one of my coworkers about how I had a short period which was very unusual because my cycle would stay on sometimes seven days. I did not think anything of it. I got lightheaded and another coworker of mine said girl you are pregnant. I am thinking to myself I am not pregnant damn; I wish you bitches stop wishing that on me! She said, "I will bet you 50.00 you're pregnant. I was like okay that is a bet.

I knew I wasn't pregnant and it has been so since I had got an abortion when I was in the ninth grade, and honestly didn't think I could even have kids anymore because I had not gotten pregnant since then. I got a pregnancy test from off the shelf not paying for it or anything and walked directly to the bathroom. I peed on the stick and one line only showed up. I took the stick out to her and said, "I want my money on payday."

She was like girl I was playing with you, just wanted you to take the test and walked away. I walked back behind the counter and said see how y'all play games. My other co-worker said let me see it, so I showed it to her, and she said, "Baby you are pregnant and this line is just light but it starting to darken up."

I snatched it out of her hand and looked at it. There the second line was darkening up a little. I passed out completely. They got me up and asked me to take a 15-minute break. My mom was called, and they told her that I had left, going to the hospital. I didn't know why they even called her. I left the store and went to my car and drove straight to the hospital. This was too much for me and I was not ready.

What was God trying to tell me? I was praying for guidance and direction but the more and more I talked to him it was like he did not hear me. I didn't know what to do. While I was at the hospital, my pressure was high and they ran all types of tests on me. I sat there on the bed and thought to myself maybe God was telling me that I needed to stay with my boyfriend but then I came to my senses.

The door opened and I thought it was the doctor, but it was my mom. I'm thinking to myself Lord you're just trying to take me out because I cannot deal with this lady right now. I was trying to redirect her into the waiting room but the doctor came in and said, "Well I know what the problem is my dear, you've been diagnosed with…. I interrupted, "Diagnosis O Lord its serious!" Pregnancy with a smile!

Pregnant, who is pregnant? You might want to check me again doc. That is not right. I'm thinking well you cannot get an abortion cause your mom is sitting right there. I was completely in denial like I had not taken a pregnancy test already. He said, "oh I am certain, and I have the proof right here in my paper. Let us have a look and see. Did you see how high your HCG levels are? I told him I did not have any HCG or THC; check that again doc seriously.

He laughed and said, "What do you want me to do? Reprint the paper for you?" I replied, "Yes go reprint the paper!" My momma said, "Pregnant! How did you get pregnant and where?" Well in my head I was thinking fucking and I had not been celibate. The doctor came back to the room and this time he had two sets of papers. I made a pouting face. He smiled showing all his teeth and said, "Do you want me to say or see?" "Both" I replied.

"You've been diagnosed with pregnancy my dear!" It was like I had become dumbfounded. "How did I end up pregnant? I asked. "You know how," replied my mom. Oh, so now you know! The doctor left and said I will be back with discharge papers. It was not even seconds later and my mom was on the phone telling my business. This pissed me off about her, I told her to stop telling people about my personal affairs. She said, "let me call Lil David." I replied, "Man don't you call him." I was like I honestly do not know what to do now. It was too much. After getting discharged from the hospital I remember getting into my car and just sitting there.

I started crying and saying Lord, I asked you for guidance and this is the answer you leave me with, a baby!" I thought maybe I'm supposed to be with him but I didn't know that it was God's way of giving me someone to love me because I had a storm headed my way and that was very rigorous.

I knew I had to spill the beans soon because my mom had told damn near my whole family. The next day, I decided to text him to let him know. With the situation going on I was not ready for a baby and neither was he. I asked him to meet up with me and he acted as if he was so busy and did not have time for me. It made me think now how we are supposed to bring a baby into this world?

If I was going to have the baby, I did not want to be a single mother, and I did not want my child to go through or deal with the same things I did growing up. I decided that I did not want the baby at that very moment. I still had a life ahead of me and for me to get where I needed to be, I had to fix myself and heal the childhood trauma that I had gone through before I could even think about it.

When we met up, he had a car full of dudes and I let him know that I was pregnant. His reaction was like okay whatever, I am going to call you and he left. I was like see that is the main reason why. His parents were excited and so was my mom. It was crazy because I've never seen her so happy, loving and caring towards me. I like the feeling, but I have to come up with this money to get rid of the baby.

Truth is I did not have it at all. I was working and trying to pay my car note, insurance, cell phone bill, and help my mom with her bills. Like it was all a bit much. I was stressing so badly that I was facing the threat of a miscarriage. Nobody wanted anything to happen to the baby. I had to take a leave from work and everything. I did not listen to anything the doctor had to say. I remember getting into an argument and telling the dad that I was getting an abortion.

His dad was like a dad to me and he talked to me and told me how much he wanted a grandbaby and to please not say or do anything like that. I was stuck and the more and more I stressed the more it affected my pregnancy. When I heard the heartbeat for the first time I was so in awe and happy about the baby and felt bad about wanting to abort it. I decided that I would just keep the baby and try to make the most of the situation because God makes no mistakes.

The further and further along I got I had to quit school. I found out that I was having a son. At that moment, I decided that I needed to do what I could fast to heal myself and get right because I could not let the little person down because I knew he was dependent on me. In a short time I did just that and so did the dad. It was like he did a 360.

The only problem I had with him at this point was he always wanted to club. I decided to put more focus on being a great mother because of the simple fact that my mom and I never saw eye to eye and I wanted things to be different with my son. I was determined to be a better mom to him than she ever was to me.

Atlantis's Advice:

If ever you find yourself in a situation where people have done you wrong. Learn to let go! Somethings are not for you to understand and it's in God's plan. Learn to keep moving forward and let God handle your vengeance. It's important to forgive people in your life – not for them but for you.

I forgave so that I could move forward but I truly was still holding on to the hurt and truly would be in uncertain times trying to make the people hurt just as much as I was hurting. Little did I know that it was only damaging me even more. I was so fixated on being better that I truly was losing myself by holding onto what God has asked me to let go of.

I was trying to map out things on my own and I should have trusted God. I reflected on my past and life generally but the truth was about to hit me like a bullet. Don't ever let life bring you down. God was about to test my faith beyond limits. Little did I know that everything that I had gone through was preparing me. I failed all the tests He had given on purpose just so I would not have to deal with everything.

The same test God gave me, I ended up getting again because God wanted me to understand that when you know better, you do better. He placed different people in my life to help guide me.

Chapter 7
Turning Point/ Plot Twist

Life is one of those experiences that can only come with time. When you experience differently, you may come across one that you may not be used to especially from the other side of a hardship. This is okay because it helps contribute to life experiences and life experiences are what make you a wiser person. You need life experiences to help you grow.

The lady at the rec told me that I had a purpose but I was still wondering exactly what my purpose was and exactly what was her reasoning. How did she know? I always wanted to be a teacher growing up and I felt that was my purpose. This purpose informed all my decisions in life from when I was a little kid and somewhere along my way, I got off course and began hanging out with some of the wrong people, making wrong choices, and being defiant.

Shortly after having the baby, God began to brew up a storm that would be the turning point in my life to help me get back on track and know his purpose for my life. I lacked faith and trust but initially, in order for me to make it through, I had to focus on God's hope and promises to help see me through and at the moment, he would reveal my purpose to me.

At this moment, God was not my focus. I was so focused on trying to be this good woman, a good mother, and having a good career to make money. I lost focus over my life when I let the hurtful and negative things that I experienced to become my circumstances. I was not my circumstances. Do not get me wrong. Most of us have no clue what we want to do with our lives.

Even after we finish school and even get a job. Me having my son was what led me to changing careers and even at that given time, being a bus monitor was not something I wanted to do. Honestly, it was something for me to make a paycheck until I could be through with school. The more I worked, the more it was clearly defined that, teaching was what I wanted for my life.

My baby was so perfect and innocent that God had handmade him Himself special for me. I was so in love with my son. I could say that was one of the proudest moments I had ever experience in my life. Although I was a first-time mom, it was not my first encounter with a child, and everything came so naturally. I chose to keep him, so his happiness and wellbeing came before everyone including my own.

I felt guilty that I had ever thought about aborting him. I didn't like anyone telling me what to do with my baby and I was overly protective of him. In fact, I did not like anyone to tell me what to do period, and this was one of those things that I really needed to work on. My son did not go anywhere unless I had to work and he was only left with the dad, grandparents, or the lady that kept me at the daycare when I was a kid.

Other than that, it was me and my baby all the time. My past traumatic experiences had me so uptight and messed up in the head.

My relationship with other people was ruined because of it and I did not care. All this time, I had fought to be in others' life and be validated; I was done begging to be loved. In my mind, I was not going to let anyone harm him.

I never stopped to think that no one is trying to hurt him, nor was my past his reality. It is always the people you least expect that try to prey on those that cannot defend (the weak) themselves and I was not allowing anyone to hurt my baby. That seemed to be the only thing going through my head at that time. I did not trust anyone with him and I freaked out every time I had to leave him.

The relationship with the dad seemed to be getting better, so I began to think maybe my son brought things together for the better. My mom was acting differently and she was being a better grand mom than the mother she ever was to me. It kind of made me jealous because I was her only surviving daughter and her baby at that. I put my feelings aside and just decided to enjoy the moment.

It was not about me anymore and I always tell myself that all that other stuff was in the past. Everything was falling into place for me. I stopped working at Walmart and started at Head Start as a bus monitor. Shortly after I started, I was working in the classroom and working the bus. I enjoyed working with the kids in the classroom and the teacher I was working with.

She inspired me to go back to school so that I could get my degree and become a full-time assistant. I went and talked to the lady that was over the teachers about how I was originally in school for general studies and how I only had on a few hours left until I finished school and was hoping I could become an assistant while in school, her response to me was, "I don't do bus monitors!" I said, "Okay then!" But that only made me want to go harder. I was going to have her job once it was all said and done. Never let anyone discourage you or hold you back in life.

I went back to the community college and got set up so I could try to finish school. That semester I was excited about returning to school and by the time I would be done, my son would start school. I would be done with my associates and that would be a memorable moment for both of us. It had to be God because my son was a blessing in disguise as he made me want and do better things for myself.

My son was a big part of me getting my life on the right path to be exactly where God wanted me to be. That was one of his purposes. I wanted to give him everything I never had growing up and in order to do this, I needed to get myself financially stable. Before my baby, I was not worried about saving money and when I got it, I would save a little and spend the rest.

I wish my aunt on my dad's side and the lady at the rec could've have met my son; also see how far I have come they would be proud of me. I passed that semester with a 3.0-grade point average. I only had two more semesters left of school and it would be off to get my bachelor's degree. I was working hard trying to save up to get myself a house because one of my goals was to build a home for my son and I from the ground up.

I had to work on getting everything that I needed to be able to do that. I was working hard to get there. One morning I was driving on the highway trying to get to work and I was hit by an 18-wheeler. My car lost control and flipped over. At that moment, the only person that came to mind was my son. If I do not make it who was going to protect him and love him the way that I did, no one.

I am not saying that no one else loved my baby but not in the way a mother can. I began panicking when the car flipped over. The airbag came out and burned my face and arms, it was a terrifying moment.

The guy in the 18-wheeler came to see if I was okay and helped me out of the car, shortly the policed arrived. My son's grandfather saw me on the highway while passing through on his way to work and stopped to make sure I was okay.

I explained to him that the truck came over in my lane and made me hit the railing and my car lost control. I got in the car with him and he took me back to my house. My body was in pain and began to stiffen up to where I could barely move my arms and legs. My kids' daddy came and said, "You don't need to go to the hospital because that's going to take a lot of your money. I'm telling you just go straight and see the lawyer."

I tell you that boy always knew exactly what to say to mess up my mood. I am in pain and here he was concerned about money when I could have been killed. That was an awful way to show his concern. I ended up going to the hospital anyway because I was in so much pain. While there, the doctors drew my blood and began to run tests. One thing about going to the hospital is that they make sure to check you from head to toe.

When my test came back everything seemed to be fine and the doctors told me that all the pain was from the airbag and me being ruffled around inside the car. I was nervous because I did not want anything to happen to me where I could not be here to protect my son. After getting discharged from the hospital I went home and laid down to try and rest up because I still had to take care of my son.

A week and some days later, I was up and ready to go back to work because I could not afford not to work. The first day I went back, I did not feel right for some reason, so I did not stay in the classroom, I just did my bus route that morning and went home. When I made it home, I tried to go to sleep but my body felt restless for some reasons. The doctor prescribed some pills for me, but I did not take them because of how bad I got addicted to them when I was in high school, so I stayed away from them as much as possible.

If people gave them to me, I would pretend to take them and throw them in that trash or tell them that I could not swallow pills. I got up and looked at them and thought maybe I could take one. It's not like before when I was going through depression, so I went to the kitchen and got a glass of water. I took the pill and went to the bathroom. Out of nowhere, I felt a sharp pain in my side. It took my breath away and brought me to my knees.

Before having my son, I never felt a purpose to live and was ready to end it all but now I was begging God to please let everything be okay with me. The pain got tighter and my eyes began to water, taking my breath away. I closed my eyes tight; I wondered if it was the pill. I relaxed my body and just laid there on the bathroom floor and slowly the pain began to ease up. I began praying because I did not know what to think. I have never experienced that type of pain before. My body had been acting weirdly since the wreck. I got up and went to the toilet to pee and after wiping myself, there was brown blood.

My period is coming on I thought, so I put on a pad and went and laid back down to get some rest. After waking up, it was time for me to go on my bus route, so I got up to go change my pad before leaving and when I wiped, there was nothing. I was so confused at this point and something was not right about the whole situation. I was so nervous and scared; my overthinking did not make the situation any better.

I began coming up with all kinds of crazy assumptions in my head. I came to my senses and said, "Let me go to this hospital so I could know for sure what was going on." I did not want anything serious to be wrong with me. Once I made it to the hospital, I called work and told them that I would not be able to make it because I was at the hospital. They ran my blood work and brought in a machine that looked sort of like a computer.

The doctor came in and told me that I was hemorrhaging. "It's the wreck that I had a week ago. I haven't been feeling the same since then." He said, "I am going to do a vaginal ultrasound since you are not that far along to see exactly where you are hemorrhaging from. I said, "Wait! Hold on Doc. What? Far along, I am not pregnant!"

"Ma'am your blood work shows that you are and the blood that was in your urine is from you bleeding internally. I must do a vaginal ultrasound to see where you are bleeding from or you could die," replied the doctor. "Say no more!" At this point, I did not know what to think. I laid back and let the man do his job. I know if you are having sex then it is a possibility you could get pregnant, but this was out of nowhere.

Like a week ago I just had a wreck and everything was fine. Nowhere in my paperwork did it say I was pregnant. I had not been having sex in weeks so how on earth did I just end up getting pregnant? I could not afford another baby. I got depressed. Here I am trying to get my life on track. I enrolled back in school which was a step in the right direction. I had a decent job that did not require me to work evenings, nor on the weekends. I was working on my credit trying to have some financial freedom, so I could provide for my son and set him up with things if something were to ever happen to me. Pregnant?

It may sound crazy, but I honestly was thinking that it was because of that wreck with the 18-wheeler when the truck hit me. Maybe it knocked that baby in my uterus. I was fairly making it with one and now here comes another one. What am I going to do with two kids? God, please help me! I don't know what I'm going to do with two kids."

The doctor said, "You're hemorrhaging badly ma'am so more than likely you will miscarry. You also need to take some days off until you do." I know it may sound bad but that was kind of a relief for me. When I looked up at the screen and saw the tiny egg. I did not want to miscarry, but I knew I was not ready for another baby.

I told my mom that I was pregnant, but I did not tell anyone else and I told her not to tell anyone my business and I meant it. My mom could not hold water, so I knew that was a negative. She was going to tell somebody even it was my brother. I said to myself if I do not miscarry this baby then that must mean it is supposed to be here but if I do then it is not.

I was not going to stress myself out about it and I left it at that. I kept quiet about the baby to my family and friends. I was honestly a little embarrassed because my baby was not even two yet and here I am popping up with another baby. It was not done purposely for sure I can tell you that. Let's be honest for a minute: having one child is much easier than I thought it would be but I began to think what if I can't handle two children.

I was more attuned to the individual emotional need of my son already born, but with two what If I can't provide it with this baby? I was trying not to focus so much on the negative because things could be much worse. Here I was complaining about having another baby when some people cannot even get pregnant.

God had spared my life when I got hit by that 18-wheeler, so right now me complaining was a bit ungrateful. It seems like the wreck had begun to make everything in my life turn upside down. I said to myself, "You got this girl, you're a great mom to Daveon, I did well with the kids at school, and you will be a great mom to the unborn. Come to think about it, what if it's that girl I wanted so badly?"

From that moment on, I was going to make the most of my situation and like the lady at the rec told me, drowning myself in my sorrow was not the way I had to keep going. You can bet your socks and shoes that I did not miscarry that baby but later in my pregnancy, I learned that I had complete previa and with the pregnancy, I would have a scheduled c section.

This did nothing but make me stress myself out. The doctor made it seem like it was life-threatening, but I felt fine. I was praying that my placenta would move so that I could have a natural birth just like I had with Daveon. The doctor had me bedridden, and she told me I needed rest.

I honestly did not think me having complete Previa was all that bad. I felt fine so I never turned the paper in to my job and I kept on working because I could not afford not to work. I told the bus driver about my condition and he said, "Why you so hardheaded?" I told him that I needed to work but I was only telling him just in case something was to happen and to take it easy on the humps and bumps.

He was so caring towards me and much like a father figure since I had been working with him. My coworkers would call him my boyfriend to make fun and it kind of got on my nerves, but hey whatever. In October, I was planning for my oldest son's birthday party. I was so excited because I got a chance to get crafty and this is one of the things that gave me peace.

I planned to have him a birthday party at Jump because he enjoyed it so much when I went to the birthday party of a former student of mine that summer. The day before his birthday party, my brother decided to take his daughter to Chucky Cheese for her birthday. I planned not to go because when I went on my bus route, the bus driver hit a pothole and it had me hurting bad, so I was scared to even do anything else.

I was not just going to drop my baby off because I still was overly protective so I decided to let him go and I would sit while my brother watched him run around with the others. Growing up, my brother and I hated each other but it seems like he began to show me that he really did love and care about me now that we are grown. Of course, it took me to act a fool for him to stop playing with me, but I was thankful for our relationship. I was in so much pain and all I needed was to take a hot bath and I would feel better; it seems like it worked for me every day.

I could not take the pain anymore, so I asked my mother to come get me from Chucky Cheese. I was hurting so badly that I decided that I was going to sit in my brother's car. We lived close to Chucky Cheese and it seemed like my mom was taking forever. I got up and started walking towards the exit.

I was walking slowly and carefully because the doctor had told me if I were to lose as much as a drop of blood I could die. My baby was kicking super hard and I felt a pop in my stomach. It hurt so badly that I stopped dead in my tracks and I tried not to move another muscle. Blood began rushing in between my legs and I squeezed them together tightly as if that were going to stop the blood from coming down.

I called for my brother and he came running. He picked me up and told his girlfriend to get the kids and lets go. She said, "You need to call the ambulance." "We ain't got the damn time to wait for an ambulance, bring ya ass!" His girlfriend and the kids hopped in the back.

I was thinking Lord please watch over my son. I do not want him seeing me take my last breath. My biggest fear was leaving him on this earth and me not being here to protect him. Lord, please do not let anything happen to my baby. I silently began to chant; I shall live and not die repeatedly. My brother wasted time finding the keys and was panicking big time.

The girlfriend shouted, "Brandon check in the seats!" He reached between the seats and found the keys. It did not even take us five minutes to get to the hospital. Once my brother left Chucky Cheese, he hit the highway and it was a straight shot. I was losing blood steadily and the ride made it even worse as it started to gush out.

I was running off my adrenaline at this point. My initial feeling that came to my mind was numb and wet. We arrived at the hospital and my brother drove up the wrong way through the side where the ambulance parked. He ran into the hospital and told the people that I need help. My sister is outside and she is losing blood, a lot of blood and she need to be rushed into the hospital.

The nurses did not think of it as that bad and they told him I would have to come in and get checked in. I was sitting in the car still and they were taking forever but finally, two nurses came out with a wheelchair to help get me inside. I heard my brother cursing them out saying, "We ain't got time for all that signing in shit my sister losing fucking blood bad!"

When they saw me, they hurried and put me in the wheelchair and rushed me straight to labor and delivery. My brother had called my kids' dad and told him where I was and that he needed to come quickly. The same brother that I thought I hated so much and that I thought did not love me was my true hero and lifesaver, and I owed him my life.

Once I was in the hospital, I looked down at my lap and saw blood flowing down to my legs; I immediately began to panic. I suffered shortness of breath and felt numb in my legs. I was in pain and on the elevator, my breathing became irregular, I told the nurse that I could not breathe anymore.

It was like I had no more breath in me and at this point, I was trying hard to breathe. She said, "But you are still breathing ma'am, you're panicking, take your time." "Lady look at all this blood I cannot breathe, I need oxygen!" They got me into a room and hooked me up to a machine to hear if the baby still had a heartbeat.

They could not find my baby's heartbeat and I began to cry. In the beginning, I was having doubts about having another baby but now I was about to lose it. The doctor said, "We are going to have to do an emergency c section. They called for an anesthesiologist, but he told them I would have to wait because he was in another room.

By that time, my kids' dad walked through the door. I felt a bit of relief seeing that he came. He said, "You have to have the baby today?" He pissed me off, I am looking at this black fucker like are you serious? Do you not see the state I am in? I replied, "Yes, damnit!" It was disappointing but I could not worry about him at that moment.

The lady gave me a paper to sign and finally they had found a heartbeat. They unwrapped me from the machine and rolled me on the bed to an operating room. While in the operating room, they transferred me from the bed onto a cold hard table, put a mask over my nose and the doctor did not waste any time; he began cutting my stomach open. The pain was excruciating, and teardrops trickled down the side of my face falling into my ear.

The gas must be fast-acting because I became mute and could not scream nor say anything. I was thinking about my son and was praying he was okay. I was thinking in my head I shall live and not die. Shortly, I closed my eyes and drifted off into a deep sleep. I was awakened by a nurse pressing down on my stomach causing me to be in agonizing pain.

It hurt so badly and my mom was right there on the other side of her. "You are a strong one!" said the nurse. I looked at her, grabbed her hand and threw it off me. "I've got to make sure you have no lumps in your stomach. We don't want you to set up and have a blood clot and die."

At this point, I had felt myself being cut open and that was worse than me cutting myself. This pain was different and unbearable. I kicked that lady and it seemed to me that the more I would move her away from me, the harder she would press my stomach, so I got up and pushed her away from me.

I began to silently thank God for letting me make it through and I was so nervous to ask about the baby because I could not stand to hear anything bad at that moment. My mom went and got my aunt and my old coworker to come help hold me down. Talk about pissed and upset, but I just stood still and let the lady press down.

They all began to talk to me at the same time and to shut them up; I asked "where is Daveon?" My mom said they sent him to the other grandparents. I instantly got depressed, who told her to make a decision like that? Daveon was my child and I wanted him there with me. I had never let my baby go stay anywhere without me.

The nurse said, "You want to go see your Babyboy before we take you to your room?" What a big relief "Yes!" I said attempting to smile. They rolled me into the NICU in my hospital bed and I got a chance to see him and he had all those tubes and a little mask on his face. It had me worried because I knew something was not right about him being hooked up to all that stuff and it was a tube inserted into his stomach.

I began to cry tears of joy because I thought my baby was dead and I was not sure I was going to make it either. The nurse said, "Don't cry right now. He seems to be doing fine and the oxygen is helping him to breathe!" It reminded me of my nephew that died. I did not know what to think but I was not going to think negatively.

When I was moved to the room, the nurse came in with the goods and I was not going to turn down any type of medication the way I was feeling. I was thinking I would be okay that night because surely the medicine was going to put me to sleep and I would have my man there to help take care of me, right?

Wrong! He told my mom to stay with me and he was going home to get some sleep in his bed because he could not get any good rest on the little couch. At that point, it hurt my feelings to know that he was not going to be by my side all the way through and was worried about getting good rest when I nearly lost my life.

If it were me, I would not want to leave his side but that was the difference between him and me. My mom said, "Oh I was staying anyway." That warmed my heart to hear her say that she asked my coworker to stay with me while she ran home but I didn't remember anything after that because the medicine that the nurse gave put me out instantly.

When I woke up the next morning, the doctor had come into the room and I was hoping he would come with good news, but unfortunately, he ruined my whole mood for that day. How can you remain positive when everything in your world is mixed with so much negativity?

The doctor told me that had my brother not taken matters into his hands that I would not have been alive. I lost too much blood and I needed to have a blood transfusion. They had to find blood for me and would get back with me later that day. Everything he said after that was kind of like a blur to me because that dark cloud was back in my vision.

I stopped him in the middle of talking because I just could not hear anything more he had to say. I wanted to go see my baby, I was worried about him and his condition at that point. Transport came with a wheelchair to take me over to see my baby. The lady at the desk in the NICU informed me that they had a schedule when I could come and visit the baby.

She told me I had to wait another hour before I could come and see him. I was pissed, exactly how are you going to tell me that I can't see my baby right now? That's my baby lady!" Ma'am, unfortunately, that is just how it is, I do apologize but the doctors are in shift change and while this is going on, you cannot be back here.

Well, their shift change doesn't have anything to do with me, I want to see my baby and I want to see him now!" Transport began to roll the wheelchair in reverse, but I quickly locked the wheels. I told the guy to stop rolling me away; I was not done talking and I have not seen my baby.

At this point, I was not thinking with my brain. I was about to throw a temper tantrum like a little ass baby. I wanted to see my baby and I was not leaving until I saw him, and I meant that. The doctor came to me very calmly and showed concern. I explained to him what happened that prior night and I did not get a chance to even see my baby.

Well I did but I was doped up, so I barely remember. He explained to me their policy and he reasoned with me and told me I could go in and look at the baby, but I could not stay more than five minutes. I thanked him because all I wanted to do was see my baby.

The guy in transport tried to help me back in the chair but at that point, I was like fuck him and that chair. It took me a minute, but I walked myself to the room where my baby was and took a seat in the rocking chair. Trying to walk was painful and made me lose my breath quickly but for some reason, I always did the opposite of what I was told.

I caught my breath and got up and washed my hands, put on some gloves, and a gown. I walked over to my baby and he was laying under a light and it was like you could see through his body. I asked the nurse to take off his mask so I can see his face. She told me she could not take it off but she would lift it so I could see his face because of the light they had on him because he had laryngitis.

When I saw his face, I began to cry and laid my head on the nurse's shoulder. The lady said it's okay we are going to do everything we can to try and get your baby home. Don't worry, we are the best NICU in northern Louisiana. I looked at the lady and said, "He doesn't even look like me!" I started crying baby tears. The nurse seemed confused. I was concerned about my baby's health, but I was upset that he looked like his daddy and that honestly hurt my soul.

The doctor told me I would have to come back within an hour to visit him properly and so I turned away and took off all the stuff I had and threw it into a basket as I walked out the door. I was crying so hard that snot was coming out of my nose. In my head, I was like okay now you're just overdoing it being crazy, it's okay Laney the baby is alive, just be thankful for that.

I covered my mouth and screamed I can't believe my baby came out looking like that man. The nurse came and she said, "Is everything okay, you honestly cannot tell who he looks like right now, but he is still precious." Ma'am, you are not helping me, I am hurting, and I need a wheelchair.

The lady backed away from me and was like let me call transport for you. In her mind, I bet she was like this lady is crazy. She didn't even have to say it because her face showed it. I can admit I was really tripping at that moment and I was still high off the gas and that medicine.

I know I freaked the lady out but honestly, I felt like a crazy woman and my emotions were all over the place. I did not even know what feelings I was feeling. The next day, I was informed that they found some blood for me which was something good to hear and would come up with the blood for me shortly.

That honestly, freaked me out and I just had to ask the lady do you know what's all in this blood, and exactly who it came from because I have two kids and I cannot just be taking blood from anybody? The lady chuckled and said, "Yes, Ma'am we have to check the blood before we even give it to you and its completely fine."

I think I had watched too many lifetime movies because I seriously was thinking the worst about everything. Those couple of weeks were hard for me to deal with because I seriously did not have the emotional support that I needed but one thing I can say is my mom never left my side.

Our relationship had gotten a little better over time. I learned that my mom did have love for me but she did not know how to show it nor did she express it. It was not the love that I needed or the love that I gave to my children and that is what I needed.

I could not drive and had to depend on my kids' dad and mom to take me to see my baby and other places. This was hard because they made me feel like I was a burden to them. My mom told me that the people at the hospital are taking care of my baby, so you don't have to run up there twice a day. She struck a nerve and some frustration that came out before I even knew it.

"Didn't you have a daughter that died? Do not tell me exactly not to go see my child. That was your problem. You never put your kids first; always some man!" I know that was hurtful, but I honestly did not care because she could not tell me anything, after all, she did not live by the advice she was trying to give me.

Here I was trying to be the mom she was not and her trying to tell me anything would instantly set me off because of the things I went through as a child. My kids' dad was telling me your mom is right, you can't be worried about one more than the other because you still have this one here, and that pissed me off even more and I let him have it also.

"You're so busy worried about running the streets all damn day and that's why you are not a real man or father figure. You like being up under your friends so much I'm starting to think y'all fucking, with your gay ass!" I meant exactly what I said but I was acting out of hurt and stress. I was abusing the pills that the doctor gave me, and I was just completely out of it.

I felt lost and I honestly did not know what to do. I wanted my baby home with me. I was not eating nor was I sleeping. I was completely overwhelmed and emotionally fragile. I was already sensitive, but you could look at me and I would begin to cry. I was trying my best to be strong because my oldest did not understand but he would always give me hugs and kisses, but even that made me feel nothing.

Since they did not want to take me to the hospital that night, I took my keys and took off. Visiting my baby brings me temporary happiness, but I just was not happy at all. One of the nurses must have picked up on my energy when I visited that night. She was extra friendly and talkative. I was hurting so badly but I was not going to be rude to her because she was in there with my baby.

I actually enjoyed talking to her and her company. The next morning, I began bleeding heavier. That was not going to stop me though. I popped those pills and waited for the daddy to come and take me to the hospital. He told me man you be tripping and what you said hurt my feelings but I did not care because it was not nearly as bad as all the shit he took me through since I had been with him.

That morning I got a report that my baby was not doing too good and they had to go up on his oxygen and all this happened overnight. The nurse told me, "You have to take care of yourself in order to get your baby home. She said one thing that I've seen mothers do is breastfeed their baby and your son probably would be home in a week or two."

I was trying but I was not producing any milk. This was incredibly stressful, and I did not know what to do, so I prayed with my baby as always before I left. I went home, cooked my son and I a full course meal and ate. At that point, it was mind over matter.

I had to stop taking the medication because I did not want it to harm my baby but as soon as I started eating and drinking water, I began to produce a little amount of milk just enough for him. Breastfeeding my baby really did work because within the next week my baby was home. I was so excited about him being home. Finally, I could get back to myself again.

My ego told me that once everything falls into place you will be at peace. In life, you learn that somethings come together only for everything to fall apart. I believe everything in life happens for a reason and this was to put me on the right path that God had in place for me. I had both of my sons home with me and I was satisfied, and now it was time for me to pick back up where I left off.

I enrolled back in school and began to work again. I enrolled Daveon into a learning Academy to try and put him in a school setting so that when he did make it to Head Start, it would not be that bad. I was trying my best to trust others and start letting him go places without me. I thought I was truly being healed from my past and moving forward.

I was ready to try and get a house, get married, and finally have my family together. This was what I wanted but God had a different plan for me. This was my plan and not His, the more and more I worked hard and was trying to get myself and the kids' father on track, the more and more it was not working. We began arguing and the more he pissed me off the more aggravated I was and it was me who started beating him.

I thought I was truly focused and on the right path, but God said, you have gone too far down and I've got to turn you around. I should have settled some things in my life long ago, but I was so fixated on how it was with my aunt and uncle that I wanted my life to be like theirs. I felt like I was too old to be living back with my mom with my two kids.

I was trying to help my kids' daddy to get his head straight but I only ended up pushing him away. I would always pray and ask God for signs and guidance, but nothing made any sense to me. Why was he not stepping up and being a man? I thought a man is supposed to be the leader, put his family first, work to provide and build together.

This boy was not doing any of that. He was still roaming the streets, clubbing and doing what he wanted to do. I finally said, "God if this is the person, I'm truly supposed to be with then it would not be this hard nor draining. I'm trying to build and he was steadily bringing me down!" I was pouring everything into him and I was not receiving anything in return.

I decided to leave him alone. I was still dealing with depression from when I had almost lost my life and the baby. I had a roof over my head, food to eat, and a job that was paying me money. I was not looking at the bigger picture, I had everything I needed. I was still feeling lost and empty even though my boys were home with me.

I felt that I was supposed to be with him, and he was what was missing. I wanted my family, so I decided that I would get back with him and let him do exactly what he wanted to do. I ignored and overlooked everything God revealed to me. We all experience storms in our lives. God had to get me back focused.

On these occasions, you may experience pain, suffering or loss. I had made the wrong choice; all this time, God was showing me that I needed to leave this boy alone and I was not going to do it so he was going to do it himself. God brought the storm in my life. Barely a month later, I found out that my job was going to be closed permanently.

I was thinking that I will just focus on school, get a part-time job and everything will be okay. It was not like I had a mortgage to pay but I did have to help around the house, and I could not just stay with my mom for free. I had to take care of my kids and I was doing most of this on my own and not the other bills that I had.

My kids' dad had gotten into a financial situation, so I was still trying to help him out and I took out a loan for $5000 to help him get back on his feet. I was thinking that if I helped him out then he would take care of me and the kids while I was going through my situation of not having a job at that moment until I got another one.

He normally would always look out for me and we always had each other's back. I should have known better than to do something like that, but I was not expecting him to do anything that would hurt me even though he was my downfall from jump. I thought maybe this was a bit of a blessing because I would have more time with my kids.

The little money that I managed to save up ran out quickly. I would always take my kids out and do fun things with them during the time I was not at school. One day my car broke down on me. I took my car to the shop and found out that my transmission was going out. This had me kind of a down because I needed a way to school and a way to get around period.

It seemed like every time I turned around it was something going wrong. I talked to my kids' dad and I told him that I had bought myself a bus pass and for the time being I would use that to get around. He didn't like the idea of me riding a city bus with kids, so I told him he could just come and get the kids and I would ride it alone.

I was on a mission and I felt like I needed to get it done because it had already been three years and at a community college, it takes you two years. My kids' dad would borrow his mom's car to get me and the kids back and forth to school for the time being. I found a used transmission at a local junkyard for my car and my mom knew the guy that worked on my car so I bought the transmission along with another part that I needed for the car and paid him to fix my car.

When I got my car back, it was still messed up so I took it back to the guy and he said he would redo it but I had to buy another transmission. I bought the other transmission spending everything that I had left on it. The guy told me he had two other cars ahead of mine so it would be a couple of weeks which was fine because I had plenty of patience and I didn't want him to rush the work and the car would not be working like before.

I got a job at the Toys R Us close by our house. I was excited to finally get something after putting in many applications. I loved Toys R Us and I was always in there buying something. I came in there so much that the lady that worked at the service desk told me they were hiring, and I took advantage of the offer. It is always who you know in Monroe to get a job, so I was grateful to always be kind and courteous because you never know when you might need the help.

It was not much but it was something to bring in some income for me until I could get to where I wanted to be. My mom helped me out a lot with my boys while I worked. My mom and I never saw eye to eye, but I was thankful that she would be there to watch them. Although growing up she left me unprotected a lot, she did the opposite with my boys.

I truly had it hard with my mom but to me, it was like she was making up for the things she didn't do for me while growing up and then I thought well, one of the reasons is that she is getting older so she has matured more. I began working and it was different because I was used to working days and not evening/nights since I had Daveon.

Not long after I started working, my mom decided to let my oldest brother move back in due to somethings he experienced with his wife and he was starting back over. This made many feelings of the past return even before he had physically moved back in. I went back and forth with my mom because I did not want him there; to visit was okay but to live no way. I did not want him around me or my boys. Here I was thinking I have forgiven him.

I thought that I was past everything, but it made me uneasy with him now living back with us. He was always his normal self but I did not want him touching my children at all. I observed him playing with them from time to time, but I did not let them get close to him or let them go into the room with him. I was often thinking about quitting because my mom would watch them while I was at work, and I just began thinking about how I was always left unattended or with someone else.

I told her not to let my kids go around him if I am not here. She would say, "I don't think he would try that now with your kids." Funny because I thought she did not recall/know he was doing that to me but anyway, I let her know that was her problem. You never think! It was kind of harsh but I just had to let her know because she did not think he would do what he did to me, but he did.

After we had that talk, she promised not to let him harm them, but it still did not sit well with him being back home. I notice how she took medication at night and it would have her out. That did not sit well with me either. When I would be home, I would not say anything but "hey" to my brother because I did not feel the need to hold a conversation with him at all.

I was never a heartless person even though he did things to me and it affected me, I still would buy food and other household materials for everyone that lived there. I would bath and take my kids to my room and close the door and put the dresser behind the door so no one could get in. I honestly had prayed to God and had forgiven him about what he had done to me but with him being in the house again I began to get restless and have horrible nightmares.

One night he knocked on the door and called my name. I pretended like I was sleep and I did not know what he wanted but I was not moving the dresser from behind my door. That dark cloud began to come back into my vision. I talked with the kids' dad and told him how I felt, and he said, "I will kill that boy if he tries something."

I told him that is why we should be looking for a house and he replied, "I'm on it." I felt a little better knowing I would finally be at peace not be around him. He told me that he was going to get his mom to put an apartment in her name for us around the corner from where she lived.

The holidays were approaching fast and I was working a lot of hours at the store. I would even take on additional shifts because once the holidays were over, I would be back out of a job since I was hired on as holiday help. My kids' dad and I seemed to be doing fine but out of nowhere he would begin to pick arguments and trip with me for no reason.

I could not take him at that moment because I had a lot on my plate and I was beginning to stress out badly. I did not understand why he was acting the way he did because I was not doing anything to him. My brother being home seriously had put me back into depression and I needed help.

I was still trying my best to make it day to day with my children. When New Year hits, I was bringing my new years in church like I did every year and my kids' dad was bringing in his new years with a whole other female. The ultimate betrayal.

Atlantis's Advice:

I want you to know that God is not going to stop every difficulty you may experience, including breakups. All my life, I searched for the easy way that would end the hurt but in these difficult times is where God was just trying to make me strong and give his everlasting grace so that I could make it through.

Life kept bringing me to the same test repeatedly because like I said before, I had not passed. The reality of my fear: I was not afraid to love; I was just afraid of not being loved back. I was not afraid of telling on my brother; I was just afraid of being ignored and my mom would not believe me. I was not afraid of the people around me; I was afraid of rejection.

I was not afraid of letting go; I was just afraid to accept the fact that he was really gone. I was not afraid to try again; I was afraid of getting hurt for the same reason. Sometimes when God is speaking, you have to learn to listen or you will miss exactly what he is showing and trying to tell you. If ever you find yourself in a situation, learn to give your problems to God.

We often say we trust God but we tend to try to fix things and mess them up. Learn to trust his plan and let go of fear. All of this time I was wondering why things were not working in my favor. My problem was the fact that I was feeding distractions. The whole time I was thinking that this is what I needed to be to do better that I ended up missing the fact that I was starving my personal focus that would really help me get to where I needed to be.

Chapter 8
Gracefully Broken

Will I ever stop having the feeling that I was cheated of something essential? Even at today's age, it makes me angry and I am grown with children of my own. I lacked confidence, found it difficult to set boundaries, and lacked trust. My trust issues came about when my mom began putting herself before me when I was a little girl.

I had grown up all my life without my mother's love, support, and protection; this left me with many wounds. I did not get it from her, so I lean so much on others to get comfort. This was a major problem. I knew that people were not to be trusted. I figured if I remain the authentic and genuine person I truly am, I would not have any worries about anyone crossing me for whatever reason.

When someone betrays you, it reflects in their character, not yours. Now I am not saying I was a victim, but I did not bother anyone unless they came bothering me. The saddest thing about betrayal is that it never comes from enemies. A lot of people do not understand why some people react immaturely or for me, I was the most difficult person to deal with, but I had my reasons for it all.

You cannot just do things and expect it to be okay, especially when my intentions were good from the start. When you have a good heart like mine, sometimes it does not see the bad. My entire life, I have avoided speaking my mind and allowed many things to go unsaid as if my feelings did not matter.

I was by far one of the most underestimated people to many, only because I was so quiet, but I loved proving others wrong. I even went on feeling like I was weak because of some of the things I endured but never underestimate the power within yourself. This was one of the advantages I had but I still had to go through a little bit more to realize it.

Trust was a big issue for me all my life. I had done nothing to that evil man, and he took advantage of my innocence. I felt betrayed by everyone and to be betrayed by people you put your trust in fully, is the most heartbreaking thing. What makes it so hurtful is the fact that the trust I had was violated by the one person I never felt as though they could do such a thing. I saw potential in my kids' dad that others always put him down.

I knew how it felt so I empathized with him a lot. My problem was I was always trying to save other people instead of helping, healing, and saving myself. I knew something was not right because since I had been in church and getting to know God for myself, I always prayed for discernment and understanding.

On New Year's eve, I set goals for myself such as things I needed to accomplish and things I needed to work on to be a better person. I started the year off trying to give myself a fresh start because every year would always end up totally different from the goals I set for myself at the beginning of the year.

It was only the beginning of the year and I was already overwhelmed. Mid-January, I was trying to stay strong but I was truly falling apart. I remember it all so well; I was at home trying to get my kids together because I had worked that same day.

I felt happy that I had got kept from the seasonal crew but I was stressing out because my checks were not enough for me to even cover at least one of my bills let alone help my mom out with the bills at the house. I was getting behind on my bills and this was not even like me because I paid my bills on time.

I could not afford to pay for the school Daveon attended anymore. The man was taking forever with fixing my car and to be honest, he was giving me the run-around. Every time I had my mom to take me there to check on the status, he would make up an excuse. It even got to the point where he would pretend like he was not at the shop.

I spent all the money that I had left trying to get that car fixed. I wanted to sue him but I did not have enough money to even get a lawyer. My problem was I paid him before he had even completed the job. School was an overload and I could not keep focus but because I was so worried about how I was going to pay my bills with nothing.

I had a lot on my plate and it was all too much for me. I went to work every day and gave it my all and still, my checks were not enough. It got to the point where I was just showing up and not even doing any work. I was applying for other jobs while I was at the store most of my shift. I began wearing my heart on my sleeve and people were beginning to feel everything I was going through. I was a totally different Atlantis and I was bringing around bad energy.

I mean nothing was working in my favor. I was miserable and I honestly would begin to isolate myself because I did not want my kids picking up on my energy nor did I want to make the way I was feeling affect someone else. After work that day, I came home that night completely exhausted. But I still could not rest because I had a paper and quiz that was due in less than an hour.

After I got out of the shower I went and got my laptop to submit my paper and start the quiz. Before I could even get started, I got a text on my phone. I decided not to check it because I did not need any distractions at that moment. I looked at my phone and it was an unknown number. I thought that was strange because I did not talk to anyone else besides family and I had no friends.

I unlocked my phone to check my messages and saw a picture of my boyfriend and a girl. My heart skipped a couple of beats. I was thinking this is the same thing that he did to me in high school. Why is he on a picture with another female in a hotel room.

To everyone else he was single but I wish he would have let me know so this would have not come as a big shock/surprise to me. I called his phone and did not get an answer. I had no car so I could not just pop up on him. I got up and took my kids to my mom's room and told her I had somewhere to go I would be back.

I called his phone until he answered it and when he finally did, he was like what did you send me that picture for?" I replied, "Come outside!" It took him forever to come outside and he knew the type of female I was. He had his daddy peeping out the window but at that point, I did not care. I said, "Why the fuck are you on a picture with this female? Who the fuck is this?"

He replied, "That's old. I was at a kick back and we took the picture, she cools nothing like that! That was when we broke up several years ago." I said, "Well why is it in a hotel room?" "That's where the kick was, tf?" I said, "This my last question and your last chance. Where the fuck is the rest of the people because I don't see anyone else in this room but you and her?"

Man, I'm not about to do this with you man you tripping that's old, I was asleep and I'm about to go back to bed. I wanted to hit him so badly but I just got into the car and left and went back home to my kids. I had missed the deadline for my work. I cried crocodile tears and I was so hurt because I wasn't expecting this again from the one person that promised, begged and put it on his grandma and cousins grave that he would not do it anymore.

I knew he was lying, and that picture had to be recent and it was not old. It really made me upset because it was like he had no respect for me at all. That boy looked in my eyes and lied to me again like it was nothing. It was like I was too stupid to him that I did not know the difference. The fact that he could stand there with a straight face hurt me even more.

After that, I reached out to his brother and a close cousin to talk to them because I know I couldn't confide in anyone else in my family except one person and I knew if I called that person, he would tell me exactly what I did not want to hear at the moment and my feelings would be hurt more than they already were.

It kind of was embarrassing but I was already dealing with enough with my financial situation, school, and now him. Pictures kept popping up and this boy kept denying it. Dealing with everything that I was going through, I felt weak. I had school, no car, a job that was paying me extraordinarily little money, and staying with my mom was nothing but stress.

I could not even provide for my children and this truly broke me down. The loan that I got in my name he stopped paying it and the people told me they were going to sue me. I had two little people that were depending on me and they were so innocent. I had to remain strong for them but I had nothing left in me.

This boy had hurt me to the core and I was still trying to hang on but the wounds were deep. I was truly down on my luck and he was back on his feet and showing his true characters like before. I had no one to lean on nor did I care to discuss anything with anyone. I desperately needed to vent but I just carried on like everything was peaches and cream.

I had remained strong for so long and pretending that nothing was going on. I knew others knew about it and they were talking but me acting as if I was okay that was my way of not talking about it at all. One day I was talking with my god sister feeling numb and hurt. Acting as if I was okay but she said one thing to me and it had nothing to do about the situation. I muted the phone and broke down crying.

I could not help it and it was completely out of my norm. I ended up hanging up the phone because I could not let her see me so hurt and vulnerable. I decided that I was going to keep moving like the lady at the rec had reminded me. I was done with drowning myself in sorrow I said to myself. It sounded good but it was easier said than done.

I finally decided to get the courage to call my uncle. I knew he was going to encourage me and tell me exactly what I needed to hear. I called him when I was in Walmart with my mom. I remember trying to talk to him and I broke down on the phone. I did not want him seeing me in that way because I never portrayed being weak at all.

I could not help it; I was hurt and so emotional. I was trying not to drown myself in my sorrow because I knew it was not my fault. The lies that he was telling me I did not believe; I was not this naïve girl like before. I just could not believe that he could look me dead into my face and lie to me like he did. The one girl that stayed by his side when he had nothing; that helped try to build him up, and show him I would be there through thick and thin.

If he did not want to be with me then I was okay with that. But I wanted the loyalty, trust and to be respected – nothing more. I would have felt better if he told me I do not want to be in a relationship with you but he was playing on my top like I was a nobody. We grew up together and he was like my best friend that I could turn to when I had no one else and he knew almost all my secrets and some of the things I had been through.

God works wonders and that ultimate betrayal is what almost took me out but saved my life and got me to the point where I am today. After talking to my uncle, he told me exactly what I needed to hear and his cousin, though she was for him, helped me get to the point where the decision I needed to make was obvious.

My uncle said, "Fuck him, you don't need him!" And his cousin said, "He told her that he did not want to be with me anymore." It was funny because every time I would talk to him it was always different. I just wanted to know why? This was not the first time I experienced betrayal but this time around it hurt me even more. I decided that I was going to let him go and try to move on with my life. I still wanted to know why and how he could treat me like that but that was the one answer I would never know.

I was in too deep. I was still trying to do my best in school and I was not focused. I was hurt behind that betrayal. I had to sometimes walk to and from school. I had no money but I still had a job. After I stopped bothering and talking to him, he reached out to me. I was at a party at a hotel that my friend hosted for her daughter.

I felt like not even texting him back, but I did anyway. He asked me where I was and I told him that I was at a hotel waiting on my mom to come pick me up. He said, "I can pick you up, just hold on." I waited for almost 30 minutes and he never showed up. I texted and called my mom but no answer. I only wasted my time waiting for him and lost my ride.

I began to walk home from the hotel by the mall. When I made it close to where Target was, he called and said, "I'm on my way. I had to find a ride." At this point, I was already walking home and it was almost midnight. I said, "Don't worry about it I have a ride." This boy was full of shit and I was wondering how I had made it this long dealing with it all in this relationship.

I had been minding my business and not even bothering him then like always but he would try to ease his way back into my life. I had made it home and took my bath. Even at that moment, I knew he was lying. I laid down because I had to work the next day. He came knocking on my bedroom window. I laid there for a while and just let him knock.

He texted my phone and said, "Laney I'm sorry for everything. I am stuck outside and I do not have a way home. Can you give me a ride home?" I knew he was lying at that point. I texted him back, "Well you can walk home, your feet are working perfectly fine. Just like mine was when I just had to walk all the way from the mall home."

He said, "I'm sorry for lying. It's just you would always try to nag me and I would always say hurtful things. I don't want to be with that girl. I messed up." I did not want to hear that shit at all because he just was a liar and it honestly was not even about the girl. He had some issues that he needed to work on himself at that point. All I wanted was to make the pain stop. It was the same scenario and the boy was not sorry.

At that point, I just wanted to focus on my kids and get myself on track and he was a liability and a distraction. He told me he had a surprise for me. He was doing his usual routine to try and get back with me. On Valentine's Day, he did the same thing that he did when I caught him cheating before. I decided to accept the gifts he gave me, and I went out to eat with him on that day.

He got us a hotel room and everything. He had another thing coming if he thought he was going to play me. He went to extreme measures to prove a point he did not have anything to do with the girl, so I went to the extreme to see how much of a liar he truly was. I said, "Let's take a picture!" He agreed to take the picture and I took it and posted it on Facebook just to see how sincere he was.

I never saw anything after that but my cousin and other people would always tell me stuff. I was dealing with him because I did not want to go through that type of hurt. I did not ask of anything from him but I was just listening to how much of a liar he was, and this boy was still making a fool out of me and I let him. We were on the phone one day and I kept hearing this noise.

I asked, "What is that noise?" He replied, "My mom got a new alarm system." I knew that was a lie because his mom and I talked all the time. She would also tell off on him and did not even realize it because he was lying to her also. He said, "That apartment is supposed to be ready at the end of this month." I told him that he could just sleep in one room and I would still sleep in the room with the boys.

At this point, I was going to focus only on me. I asked him about paying that loan and he told me he was behind but still paying it. Just talking to him made me depressed. I was not happy and I did not know what I needed to do to change it. In the beginning, I felt like we were supposed to be together but he began to disgust me.

I felt so alone and I started pushing my kids away and leaving them with my mom a lot. I felt like my kids were better off without me. That day, I hung up the phone on him and it was different. I was thinking maybe if I moved out, I would not have to deal with the stress of my mom because I was not making enough to pay her bills. I put food in the house, bought toiletries, washing powder, etc. That was not enough for her.

I even told her I needed help and her response to me was you can't live here and not pay bills. She felt like I had money but I honestly had nothing. If it was not for her, I would not have a place to lay my head. She did not want to take me anywhere and I was putting gas in her car. At the time I was hurting, I knew I needed the love and support of my mom but she only made it worse.

Who else was going to let you come and live with your two kids? I did not know when I would get back on my feet. I was trying to remain focused but I could not help but be depressed. I prayed and asked God for strength because I needed it badly. I was hesitant about going to live with the kids' dad because he had already put me through enough.

Trying to help him out always put me in a position to lose every time. I was counting on him to help me take care of the boys and to help me get back on my feet. He was making money because he would always flash it showing me on facetime. It made me think; how are you supposed to be a man when you cannot even help your own. How can you let the mother of your kids struggle?

One day I was working the evening shift at the customer service desk. I was cleaning and zoning the area because we had little customers in the store. A police officer walked in along with a lady to the service desk. "Hi, welcome to Toys R Us. Can I help you?" The lady turned around and said, "Yes, I'm looking for Atlantis Brown."

"I am she, what can I do for you?" The police turned around and that made me nervous because I know I did not do anything, but it made me uneasy. "The lady said, "Ma'am we have been trying to contact you about your title loan. Mr. David is not returning our calls and has not been able to make payment in three months." She showed me some documented papers and the title to my car.

I said, "Okay I got the loan to help him out and he assured me that he would pay it. Why did you get the officer involved?" She replied, "Ma'am this is a legal matter. I was thinking my mom had got plenty of loans and they never called an officer on her. I had a customer and this shit was so embarrassing. I said, "Give me a minute!" While I was checking out the customer the lady said, "We are going to have to sue you for the amount you owe and she asked me where my car was?"

I tried to ignore her so I could get the customer out of the store. "Where is the black Honda accord ma'am?" I did not know what to do and had never experienced anything like that in my entire life. After checking out the customer I said, "Let me call him." He just had shown me a stack of cash on facetime. I called from my phone several times and did not get an answer.

I even called from Toys R Us phone and no answer. The lady said, "We came to collect the car?" I told her that I put the car in the shop because the transmission was out. The lady said, "I need the address." "Look I'm not lying to you I know where the shop is but I don't know the address, can you give me some days and I can come up with the money. I need my car."

Unfortunately, we have let this loan go past the due date and I can't do that anymore. You can pay the amount in full and then we won't have to take your car or file these papers." I said, "I will be in tomorrow with the money before you all close." "We close at 7!" said the lady and turn and walked away. "You have a good day ma'am," said the officer and followed behind her.

White sons of bitches, a good day I said to myself. I was not focused and I could not reach this dude at all. It was almost closing time and he texted me saying what is up? Now I know he received all those calls and messages I left. I called him from the store phone trying to explain everything that just happened.

He said, "Those people just be stunting, they ain't going to do anything. I'll call you back, I'm handling something," and hung up the phone. Now I would have never left him in a position like this and he showed no concern. This was truly hurtful. In the car ride on my way home, I desperately wanted to talk to my mom and just cry on her shoulder.

While at home all she did was go on and on about the bills, how all my kids did was mess up the house and how she was not a maid. I did not understand how you sit and let them mess up this whole house; you must not be watching them. That really set her off because she went on and on saying how I took my money and did whatever I liked with it. How was that when I bought everything for the house and put the food in there. I did not have enough money to even pay one bill.

I need help and their daddy was not helping me at all. That night I wanted to take a ride, so I told my mom that I was going to get something to drink at the store and ended up at my god sister's house. I just needed someone to talk to not about my problems but just a friendly conversation. I did not stay long because I knew she would be wondering where I was at.

On my way back to my mom's house I got a call from the kids' dad and he was saying that he was going to have his mom make a payment tomorrow. I just said okay and once again I heard that chirping noise before he hung up. I got a feeling and something was not right about the whole situation. I had spoken with his mom and she was at home and I did not hear one chirp.

Something told me to ride out to where those apartments where and I followed my instincts. When I made it out there, I drove to the apartment that he said we would be getting which was on top of his brother's and girlfriend at the time apartment and I saw his brother and his mom's car. I said this boy is a fucking liar. I already knew but the fact that he tried to run that same game on me but I knew better to go for it.

Why lie about getting an apartment for us when I'm certain he already had it? I drove my mom's car and parked it on the other side of the apartment complex and walked back over to that apartment and started to beat on the door. It took a minute but eventually, he came out saying "you're going to get me put out." I said I don't give a fuck about you getting put out. Here I am struggling about to get sued and you're living in a whole apartment with the female you claim not to even be talking to.

I said, "All you do is fucking lie, it made no sense." He called his dad on the phone but I did not give a fuck at that point. I never asked him for one thing, why would you even try to play on my top like that. If it were not for me getting rewards at Toys R Us, my baby would not even have pampers. How can you sleep at night? Stop trying to play me like I do not take care of my kids.

Well, you fucking do not! He was doing whatever he liked with his money. All of a sudden, he just stopped doing and he tried to make it seem as though it was because I always tried to play him but you cannot argue with someone that believes their own lies because in their mind they are always right.

I was better off not even knowing and something told me not to drive out there but if something didn't sit well with me, I have to know. We started fighting outside the door. He said, "I'm going to take you to my dad, I don't have time for this!" "What the fuck is your dad going to do to me?" I walked down the stairs and got into the car, but I only got in because I wanted to fuck with him.

While he was driving, I kept switching the gears, punching him and trying to get out of the car; just acting a plum nut. I told him that I wanted to go home. He turned the car around and he started driving me home. Halfway there, I told him that I needed to go back and get my mom's car. He said, "Why are you doing this?"

I slapped him dead in his face and said, "That's why just take me back to my mom's car so I can go home. He said, "I'm taking you to my daddy." At that point, I did not even care. I dropped my mom's keys because I did not have the strength to do anything else, I just sat back and rode. I began to cry, here I was with nothing and it was all because I was too busy trying to help him get on his feet and when he got on his feet the boy did not do anything he had promised.

I lost the house I had because of him, I was about to lose my car because of him and I was about to be sued because of him. My mom wanted to put me out and the job I had wasn't okay because my checks were not enough. I just could not deal with all of this anymore. I could not even take care of my kids and that made me feel less of a woman.

This boy broke me down to my lowest and I truly had nothing. On the way back he was trying to talk to me but whatever he was saying I did not even hear. I switched cars and got into the truck with his parents. They were talking to me and I just had told them everything about how their son had lied, he was not helping me with the kids, he had not paid the loan and the people were talking about suing me.

I looked at my phone and it was three in the morning. I checked my account and my check had hit. When we made it to my house their son was there, and I did not know why and my mom was waiting outside. She said, "Why are you acting crazy?" I walked past her, went inside the house and got my pm pills and I kissed my babies. I asked his parents if they could take me to a nearby hotel so I could just get myself together.

I did not want my kids to see me like this. They said, "Are you sure you going to stay at the hotel?" I said, "I don't have a car or anything else so how was I going to move to the hotel?" I was known to take off walking but I was tired. I had nothing left in me. I stood there thinking all my life I had been fighting against myself.

His mom walked up to me and hugged me so tightly and I began to try to get her off me but she just held me. That was what I wanted from my mom but it was like she hated me or something. After leaving my house they dropped me off at one of the hotels close to the mall. I got out and I did not turn around to look back.

I checked in at the front desk and got a room. When I made it to my room, I took off my shoes and laid across the bed for a couple of hours. All that toddler acting had worn me out and I was ready to check out of this world for good. I had endured enough and if this is what it was all about, then it just was not for me and I was tired of going through things.

I could not remember a time in my life where it was simply good for a long period. I truly had pretended all my life to be happy and I was done pretending. I begin to think and all my life, I had this negative self-image of myself; I felt worthless, hopeless, helpless, and I wanted the pain to be over for good. I said, "Lord I think you gave me the wrong journey."

I took the pills out of my pocket and I looked at the bottle and there were only six to seven pills inside it. I poured every single pill inside my mouth and drank some water out of the sink to make them go down my throat. I took one of the sheets and I wrapped one end around my neck and pulled both ends at the same time. I began to choke myself with the sheet.

The harder I pulled the harder it was for me to breathe. At that moment I was thinking. What are you doing girl? The sheet began to block my airway and I could not breathe. I remember my head feeling like it was about to explode and my veins were popping out. I felt like I had to throw up but the sheet kept it from coming up. I heard something say, "Just Let Go!" I pulled harder one last time.

You have two boys; you are being a bit selfish. I blacked out and I saw myself in a casket at my funeral. My boys were crying! Why would you leave them like that? They would be hurt the most. It was like I was stuck and I could not open my eyes. I thought, "Lord, forgive me for hurting my boys." Suddenly, I gagged and threw up all the pills.

Which was crazy because I drunk more than enough water to make them go down. I gasped for my breath and began choking. My body was weak, and I had no energy. I could not even open my eyes. I was trying to get myself back up. I stood up but my body collapsed to the floor with my eyes agape. I blinked and stared up at the ceiling. I swallowed hard, trying to push the nerves back down my throat.

My eyes wet with tears; I began to unwrap the sheet from around my neck. I attempted to sit up and a great sob escaped me. I covered my face with shaking hands as the sound of wailing and suffering echoed throughout the hotel room. At that moment, I sensed God's presence with me inside the hotel room. My body was filled with chills. Although He was not there physically, He was there spiritually.

This is the day that God and his angels were in a spiritual battle over my life. At that moment I was exhausted. I had given up on life completely and ready to throw it all away. I had been carrying this load of problems that were weighing heavy on my soul. You have a purpose and this is not the end of your story. I instantly went into a deep sleep.

Atlantis's Advice:

Never throw in the towel. There is a purpose for your pain. Some pains are for a lesson while others are for redemptive suffering. You may not understand nor does it make a bit of sense. Why did I have to go through half of the stuff I did when I did not do anything to anyone? Somethings you go through is to help benefit another person.

The very thing that you hate, God can use for the good in your life. What you need to understand is that the pain you endure is your purpose. Who can better help someone than a person that has experienced the same thing? Allow yourself to find semblances of peace, heal, and leave your past behind you because the purpose of your past was to teach too many lessons.

Every level in life will demand a different version of you. Holding on to the past will only stop you from going forward. You cannot go into the future with that same attitude and way of thinking. Never be afraid of change and even though you may lose something good, it will be for the better. Your story ends in victory!

Chapter 9
Ready For Overflow

Nevertheless, we often struggle to bring up suicidal thoughts with those we love. Many people that do not have any personal experience would say the person is crazy. We live in a society where everyone portrays strength and perseverance. Not everyone is born "in" the same circumstances and some people's journey is indeed harder than others. Many do not have that strong support system.

Suicide is a way out for some people and I was almost a victim of it. I feel if I had never experienced some of the things I endured; I would not be the strong person I am today. After I attempted suicide, I vowed to never try to take my life again. When it's time to leave this earth, then God Himself would have to come down and get me.

I love my boys with all my heart and soul. What would life be like for them without me? I vowed to never do anything to hurt them, but I was at a low point in my life. I always wanted to protect them and if I had taken my life, no one would be here to protect or love them as much as I would do.

Majority of that day I cried a river of tears and I cried to the point where I had no more tears left inside of me. Here I was drowning myself in sorrow. I felt bad because I told the lady from the rec that I would not do anything like this again. I wanted to be sure to get it all out. I got up from the hotel bed and went into the bathroom.

I stared at myself in the mirror for quite some time. Finally, I got my shoes and put them on. Then I walked out of the hotel and walked home to my boys. When I made it home, they were happy to see me and I was happy that I was still here. I sat down on the couch. I began to think, how can you let a weakness stop you for so long from going on?

You must do away with the wounded child within. Every time I would go through things, I would find myself deep in despair, but it never solved anything. At this moment, I took it all in because it was time for me to transform all the anger, sadness, and fear that I had been holding in. I was truly at my weakest point but right now, I had no choice but to be strong. Being strong was my only option.

I was going to adjust myself to how it was and I became resilient. For so long I knew that for you to move forward, you needed to forgive and heal. My problem was I would say it but deep down, I never forgave nor was I healed. I guess I was saying it and trying to convince my mind of that fact and make myself believe that I did.

I took a moment to tell God from this point forward that I am truly trying to forgive and let all this go. I wanted to let go of the betrayal of my kids' dad, the hurtful things I experienced with my mom, brother, and so on. I knew that God already knew about all my traumatic experiences but I wanted to present Him with the fact that I was acknowledging it myself.

I knew it was not going to be an easy process, but I did know that I was a part of the problem and it started with me. I got up off the couch and went outside with my oldest son to throw football with him. Later that day, the mailman came. I knew it had to be God because I got a letter in the mail from my 401-k from my job at the Head Start.

I had no worries because God was showing me right then that he was going to take care of my worries. My old job took money out along with myself from the time I started until the time they closed the school down. That made me happy and I took the letter up to the people at the loan company. I sat down and talked with the lady about my situation.

I told her that I am not that type of person and asked her if she would work with me being that I would now be the one paying back the loan. I showed her the paper and promised to pay when I got the money. I went to work that evening and I had a talk with one of the coworkers about my situation which was something I normally did not do and she talked with her sister and helped me get on with this sitting company.

It was like my world went from being upside down to right side up within a matter of hours. I did not always have it good, but I learned that it started with me. I had to create my happiness and I was determined to do so. The best way to move forward is to let go of the people holding you back. It was hard to move on if you do not forgive.

All the things that I had moved past and forgotten about came back. This was my way of healing the child trauma, but it did not work. I wanted to be free from pain in my body and mind. I stopped setting goals at the beginning of the year and instead, decided that I would set a goal for each day and accomplish it. I had a lot of wounds and I knew it would be a long process but I need healing. The only thing I could do at this point was to uncover those wounds, go through the hurt, and process it out.

I was determined to become a better me. I was determined to claw my way out of being so depressed. I began reading a lot of self-help books. I thought that forgetting and not talking about it would help, but it only drove me crazier.

I started conversing with other people and when it came to me, if they show me one little thing, they had to go. I was not about to let anyone interrupt the little peace I have. I was not about to play when it came to me and what I deserved. I mainly just wanted the conversation just to have someone to talk to, which was something I normally did not do.

One day, I went to sign my son up for the new upcoming Head Start and while I was there, I saw a couple of my former co-workers and was told I should put in an application. I did not think I would get hired because I was not done with school, but I decided to put my application in.

One day at school, I had gotten a call about an interview. I went for the interview and I got the job. I was so happy. Taking care of children is my passion. I have always dreamed of having a school of my own so I could protect the innocent children. This was my way of not having to deal with the trauma in me by protecting them.

When I officially started working at Head Start, I still was working for Toys R Us and let the sitting job go because I did not have my car still to get back and forth. I had one more semester of school and then my student teaching. I was beginning to be in my prime. I let God handle my vengeance for all the wrong I was done and that paid off well.

Working at Head Start could have been the best thing for my life at that moment. I had different coworkers and two of them stuck to me more than I expected because I really do not associate with many people because I did not trust them. One of them was so strange and I felt comfortable around her like I had known her my whole life.

With her, I would just talk and talk so much that it became exhausting for me to talk. I even confided in her some of the things I went through and it felt natural and I could be my normal self and we always enjoyed good vibes when we were together, which was the way I liked it. She was truly my soulmate, No drama at all and she was always a big help to me being a better me and I love her beyond words.

Then there was also p, we ended up in the classroom working together and she became my family; more like a big sister and we clowned every day at work. Working with young children is one of the most rewarding things. I get so attached to the children and have a natural love for them as if they are mine. In 2018, everything started to turn in my favor.

I began my student teaching and I finished with an A. I needed a decent car and I didn't have anyone to help me get a car so I decided to take a step out on faith and being that I did not have a cosigner, I just knew I was not going to get the car. My credit was all messed because I was helping other people out who would not help if the shoe was on the other foot, but it's funny how God work.

I got a call from the lady at the bank and she said when can you come in, so we can discuss your loan? I told her I would be in when I got off work because I never liked to miss a day with the kids. When I made it there, she said, "You don't have a long history of credit but I see you manage to keep up with your payments and you're in good standings with them all.

My credit score was a 650 and she was like you need to work on building that up. I was like oh well, I guess I will settle for a cash car but I had to make sure I would not have to deal with any shade tree mechanics. She said, "Now the car that you are trying to get will not work; it has too many miles on it. Go to the car lot and pick a new car and get them to fax me over the buyer's order."

"What? I could not just believe what that lady had told me, I was like you want me to pick any car?" She replied, "Not just any car, pick a decent one!" with a smile. I was speechless. She said, "I can tell you have had it hard and you deserve everything that God has in store for you!" I could have kissed the lady's ten fingers and toes.

I felt like that was God speaking through her because I never told her I was having a hard time or anything that would require her to feel sorry for me. I told her that I was going to school to become a teacher and talking so much about my kids and my babies at the school, just really bragging. It was so funny to me because every time I would try to get a car in my name for my kids' dad something would always go wrong, or the note would be high.

Right then and there I knew that it was only God protecting me. Seeing that he did not do right with the loan, I just could imagine what it would have been like if I had a car in my name. I left the bank and went over to the Honda dealership and I found a nice all-white Honda that was perfect for my boys and I. I was super excited; I was so thankful because nearly a couple of years ago I was a lost soul trying to find my way.

My mom and I do not have the best relationship now but even our relationship is getting better. I don't feel comfortable talking to her about anything because all this time I felt that my mom did not love or care about me. But it had a lot to do with things she had not healed from before having children. You must learn to heal the broken kid in you so that others will not get the whiplash from it.

It's ironic, now I am teaching her how to heal and deal with many things. In May, I walked across the stage and got my associates degree.

I could have not been prouder. After graduating from school, I got a promotion to be the lead teacher and I have been doing exceptionally well ever since. I love being a teacher; you get to see the real Atlantis when you entered inside my classroom.

I always wanted to be a teacher because I wanted to help children and mainly the ones like myself that had no one to turn to when all hope is gone. My first year of teaching set somethings in motion for me. Yes, I am young but I felt like I had already wasted too much time on everything else. I was my focus. I was determined that I was going to start my empire and live out all my dreams.

I owe this to myself and my children. I have always been more of a motivator to people. It seems like I attract mainly broken people but I always find myself encouraging being the one true person and doing the things I so desperately needed when I was younger. You would be surprised at how many ladies that I have met and they have experienced something traumatizing like I did.

I have always created a haven for others in myself. Their secrets are safe with me but we work together to heal the brokenness in one another. This led me to the startup of my nonprofit for girls and women. Funny because I found purpose in my pain and never in a million years would I think that I would be where I am today.

I improve something about myself every day. I am working on building my nonprofit for girls to promote empowerment through healing so they can move forward in life and become their best selves. I let go of all the toxic past and negativity and focused more on the positive. Now I am finally at a place in my life where I am walking towards my destiny and that is being the woman that I was truly destined to be.

I am on my way to my destiny!

Atlantis's Advice:

What you focus more on will determine what your outcome will be in life. Learn to replace your fears with trust so you can overcome them. You also become what you continue to do. Make a commitment to yourself and stop making excuses. Choose good habits and watch how your behavior change.

Whenever you don't understand what's happening in your life, remember things work out for the good of those who love the Lord. There is no need to stress or worry; somethings that may not work out in your favor is God protecting you. God's timing is always perfect, and anything under God's control is never out of control.

I will not lie; my journey was hard and there are somethings I chose not to share, but there is always someone that has it way harder than you. Always be grateful and thankful. In your times of weakness pray to God for strength to see you through. All my life I have portrayed a certain type of image. The sad thing is, you never know what a person is going through or how bad they are hurting.

In spite of everything I was going through, I was always kind to others and would be helpful in any way I could. I had my own way of dealing with unimaginable pain, so that I could go without being judged by others. Try refraining from judging someone because you don't know the whole story. I have survived it and finally came to a point where I could speak out about it to help heal the inner me that's been broken. In my life, it's all about perseverance. No matter the obstacles or my circumstances, I PRESSED ON!!!!!!

A Word to my sisters..................

A strong woman is both soft and powerful. Sometimes doing things that are best for you will come at a cost, but in the long run it will put you on the right path and you will be much happier with yourself. At the age of 6 is when my life changed which seem for the worst. Everything seemed to be different and to me seemed like it would never get better for me. I lost myself at an early age. I notice that many coloreds do not openly discuss these stories. We know it happened; we just do not discuss it. Our generation needs to change that. I struggled with depression and anxiety in my adolescent and teen years. Those that were close to me would have said, "There is nothing wrong with her!" Had I been properly guided and known what I know now as an adult I would have been in a much better place and enjoyed my childhood. I genuinely believe that a woman must first heal herself, find herself, know herself, correct herself, respect herself, be herself, and love herself so that she will not bleed on others. I was not just dealing with my traumas but also my mom's traumas. I heard all my life as a child you do not know anything, you do not have feelings, or you are just a kid. All the negatives. A child is the smartest person known to man. Little do you know that their adolescent years are the most vital. Kids absorb everything like a sponge. If you forecast bad things, kids prove you right. If you mock or make fun of them, kids internalize it. I have been on the path to heal myself deeply to be the best version of myself and the best person I can be for my children. I know for certain that the absorption ability work both ways. If you encourage children, they become heartened. If you speak greatness, children will work hard to achieve it. Whether they are your kids or others encourage and affirm and more importantly be an effective leader to help bring about the change that this world so desperately needs. As an educator is it my one true passion to help build a solid foundation to bring children up in the proper way. I am their teacher first, but also a mother and friend. Through my nonprofit my purpose is to promote empowerment through healing to bring together an intergenerational group of women to bring about social change. As you read, I hope to inspire you. This is my journey that I share with you. I am proud of how far I have come thus far; I have changed so much about myself and I am still growing. I went through redemptive suffering to better help someone else. I live to share my testimony with others and fight for a righteous cause. No matter what obstacle you face, you are not your circumstances, and you are not what is going on in the world. Let us talk about depression, anxiety, and suicide so people will know they are not alone, they are loved and cared for, and someone will miss them. The more we talk about it the more we empower others to say "Actually, I'm not okay!" Whenever you do not understand what is happening in your life always remember all things work for the good of those who love God. There is no need to stress or worry. Never give up! Be strong and courageous. God's timing is the perfect timing and anything under God's control is never out of control. Somethings may not be working in your favor, but never look back always KEEP MOVING FORWARD!!!! Fight the good fight and KEEP PRESSING ON!!!!!

Atlantis Brown

About the Author:

A strong woman is both soft and powerful. Sometimes doing things that are best for you will come at a cost, but in the long run it will put you on the right path and you will be much happier with yourself. At the age of 6 is when my life changed for the worst. Everything seemed to be different and to me seemed like it would never get better for me. I lost myself at an early age. I notice that many people of color do not openly discuss these stories. We know it happened; we just do not discuss it. Our generation needs to change that. I struggled with depression and anxiety in my adolescent and teen years. Those that were close to me would have said, "There is nothing wrong with her!" Had I been properly guided and known what I know now as an adult, I would have been in a much better place and enjoyed my childhood. I genuinely believe that a woman must first heal herself, find herself, know herself, correct herself, respect herself, be herself, and love herself so that she will not bleed onto others. I was not just dealing with my traumas but also my mom's traumas. I heard all my life as a child you do not know anything, you do not have feelings, or you are just a kid. All the negatives. A child is the smartest person known to man. Little do you know that their adolescent years are the most vital. Kids absorb everything like a sponge. If you forecast bad things, kids prove you right. If you mock or make fun of them, kids internalize it. I have been on the path to heal myself deeply to be the best version of myself and the best person I can be for my children. I know for certain that the absorption ability work both ways. If you discourage children, they become hardened. If you speak greatness, children will work 136 hard to achieve it. Whether they are your kids or others encourage and affirm and more importantly be an effective leader to help bring about the change that this world so desperately needs. As an educator is it my one true passion to help build a solid foundation to bring children up in the proper way. I am their teacher first, but also a mother and friend. Through my nonprofit my purpose is to promote empowerment through healing to bring together an intergenerational group of women to bring about social change. As you read, I hope to inspire you. This is my journey that I share with you. I am proud of how far I have come thus far; I have changed so much about myself and I am still growing. I went through redemptive suffering to better help someone else. I live to share my testimony with others and fight for a righteous cause. No matter what obstacle you face, you are not your circumstances, and you are not what is going on in the world. Let us talk about depression, anxiety, and suicide so people will know they are not alone, they are loved and cared for, and someone will miss them. The more we talk about it the more we empower others to say "Actually, I'm not okay!" Whenever you do not understand what is happening in your life always remember all things work for the good of those who love God. There is no need to stress or worry. Never give up! Be strong and courageous. God's timing is the perfect timing and anything under God's control is never out of control. Somethings may not be working in your favor, but never look back always KEEP MOVING FORWARD!!!! Fight the good fight and KEEP PRESSING ON!!!!!

Interested in Writing and/or Publishing your own book?
Visit @ www.A2ZBookspublishing.net

www.ingramcontent.com/pod-product-compliance
Lightning Source LLC
Chambersburg PA
CBHW072020110526
44592CB00012B/1386